CONTENTS

T0015215

Library of Congress Cataloging-in-Publication Data

Names: Hone, Trent, author.
Title: The battle of Guadalcanal / Trent Hone.
Other titles: Naval history magazine.
Description: Naval history special edition. | Annapolis, MD : US Naval
    Institute, [2022]
Identifiers: LCCN 2022000771 | ISBN 9781682477311 (paperback)
Subjects: LCSH: Guadalcanal, Battle of, Solomon Islands, 1942–1943. | World
    War, 1939–1945—Campaigns—Solomon Islands. | World War,
    1939–1945—Naval operations, American.
Classification: LCC D767.98 .H663 2022 | DDC
    940.54/265933--dc23/eng/20220203
LC record available at https://lccn.loc.gov/2022000771

INTRODUCTION

THE SIX-MONTH-LONG CAMPAIGN FOR THE ISLAND OF GUADALCANAL, fought in the lower Solomon Islands, was the turning point of World War II in the Pacific. Although the Battle of Midway in June 1942 had reversed the tide of Japanese victories, it was triumph in the attritional struggle in the South Pacific that secured the initiative for the United States and its allies. That process began with the first offensive—Operation Watchtower—which seized Guadalcanal's airfield and the anchorage at Tulagi in August 1942.

Serene at the time this striking photograph was taken (21 November 1942), these waters had been the scene of heavy activity by American and Japanese forces battling for strategic control of the Solomon Islands. Cape Esperance, Guadalcanal, is at the extreme left while Savo Island is in the center background. The view is looking approximately west. (U.S. Naval Institute Photo Archive)

UNITED STATES NAVAL INSTITUTE

Dubbed "Operation Shoestring" because of limited preparations and inadequate supplies, the effort to maintain the tenuous hold on Guadalcanal was a lengthy struggle. It began with U.S. Marines landing on 7 August and continued until 9 February 1943 when the island was finally secured. In the intervening months, the Japanese committed 36,000 soldiers and naval troops to the fighting; some 20,000 were killed or captured. Admiral Chester W. Nimitz, commander of the U.S. Navy's Pacific Fleet and the Pacific Ocean areas theater of operations, cycled 60,000 Marines and soldiers through Guadalcanal. The bulk of the fighting was done by the men of the 1st Marine Division and the U.S. Army's Americal Division; a total of 1,592 American troops were killed in action.

U.S. Navy losses were far higher. The Guadalcanal Campaign was a three-dimensional conflict; its centerpiece was the island's airfield, named "Henderson Field" in honor of Major Lofton Henderson, USMC, who died leading his dive-bombing squadron against the Japanese at Midway. Possession of Henderson Field allowed the U.S. garrison to dominate the daylight skies above the island. Japanese forces tried to disable the airfield with aerial attacks and naval bombardments. The Navy fought to prevent these efforts and to thwart Japanese attempts to land men and supplies on Guadalcanal. These "Tokyo Express" runs triggered a series of night surface battles in the waters near Guadalcanal.

These battles were some of the most furious, confused, and chaotic in the history of naval warfare. Although a few were fought by the light of the moon, most took place on dark nights in conditions of poor visibility. Passing squalls and thunderstorms obscured the movement of ships and disrupted formations. Searchlights, starshells— powerful flares fired from naval guns that slowly descended on parachutes—and the flashes of gunfire blinded participants and

Admiral Ernest J. King, Chief of Naval Operations and Commander in Chief, U.S. Fleet. He recognized the potential offered by the victory at the Battle of Midway and pushed for an early offensive at Guadalcanal. (National Archives)

made it difficult to distinguish friend from foe. The officers and men of the Imperial Japanese Navy (IJN) brought well-honed skills and sharp-eyed lookouts that compensated for the U.S. Navy's use of radar. So many ships were lost in the fighting that American sailors dubbed the nearby body of water "Ironbottom Sound."

The night battles were decisive. In three crucial engagements in October and November 1942, the Navy prevented the IJN from achieving its strategic goals of destroying the airfield and bringing substantial reinforcements to the island. Desperate actions by determined sailors and their officers preserved the tenuous hold on Guadalcanal and led to victory in the campaign. The cost was high: of 19 ships committed to the defense of Henderson Field in mid-November nine were sunk and six were seriously damaged. Victory in these actions, when it came, resulted from the Navy's aggressive tactical doctrine and individual acts of heroic leadership.

STRATEGIC SITUATION

Operation Watchtower was initiated by Admiral Ernest J. King, who had become the Navy's commander in chief (COMINCH) after the surprise attack on Pearl Harbor in December 1941. King immediately recognized the opportunity created by the victory at Midway. He resolved to strike the Japanese before they could absorb their losses and prepare for another offensive. However, King's determination for an early move in the Pacific ran counter to U.S. strategy. The Joint Chiefs of Staff (JCS), including King, U.S. Army General George C. Marshall, and U.S. Army Air Forces General Henry H. Arnold, had agreed to focus on "Germany first" and prepare for an offensive in Europe as soon as possible. However, King believed the opportunity was too important to miss; in late June, he ordered Nimitz to prepare to seize Tulagi in the Solomon Islands. With the preparations already under way, he presented

Vice Admiral Robert L. Ghormley commanded the South Pacific Area from 17 May 1942 to 18 October 1942 and oversaw the initial offensive operations at Guadalcanal. (National Archives)

Admiral Isoroku Yamamoto, commander of the Imperial Japanese Navy's Combined Fleet. Yamamoto launched a series of complex plans to overwhelm the defenders of Henderson Field and retake Guadalcanal. (National Archives)

The light cruiser *Tenryū* in a heavily retouched photograph from the 1920s. The *Tenryū* escorted the first Japanese troops to Guadalcanal in July 1942 and returned the night of 8-9 August as part of Vice Admiral Gunichi Mikawa's striking force. (Naval History and Heritage Command)

Vice Admiral Gunichi Mikawa, commander of the Eighth Fleet. Mikawa personally led the mixed cruiser-destroyer force that achieved the stunning victory at the Battle of Savo Island. (Naval History and Heritage Command)

UNITED STATES NAVAL INSTITUTE

the plan to the JCS, informing them he would proceed with or without their concurrence. Marshall and Arnold consented and agreed to the plan on 2 July.

Within days, radio intelligence revealed the Japanese had landed airfield construction troops on Guadalcanal and a reconnaissance plane flying over Tulagi noticed that the Japanese had begun clearing ground for an airfield near Lunga Point. The airfield immediately became the main objective. Vice Admiral Robert L. Ghormley, appointed Commander, South Pacific area, on 17 May, would oversee the offensive from his headquarters at Nouméa, New Caledonia. Rear Admiral John S. McCain, Ghormley's air group commander, used his planes to scout for the invasion forces. Vice Admiral Frank Jack Fletcher, who had commanded task forces at the battles of Coral Sea and Midway, would lead the attack force, which included the three carriers *Saratoga* (CV-3), *Wasp* (CV-7), and *Enterprise*

(CV-6). The amphibious assault would be led by Rear Admiral Richmond Kelly Turner. He would deliver Major General Alexander A. Vandegrift's 1st Marine Division to Lunga and Tulagi. Initially planned for 1 August, the landings were delayed until 7 August to allow time for more thorough preparations.

In the meantime, Admiral Isoroku Yamamoto, commander of the IJN's Combined Fleet, was shoring up the defenses of his southern perimeter. He expected to resume the offensive and seize Fiji and New Caledonia as part of the "FS" Operation. Their capture would sever the supply line between Australia and the West Coast of North America. Operation FS originally was scheduled to take place after the Battle of Midway, but the defeat put the plan on hold. In the meantime, the airfield on Guadalcanal was expected anchor the southern flank and provide an important stepping-stone for future offensives.

South Pacific Bases in August 1942

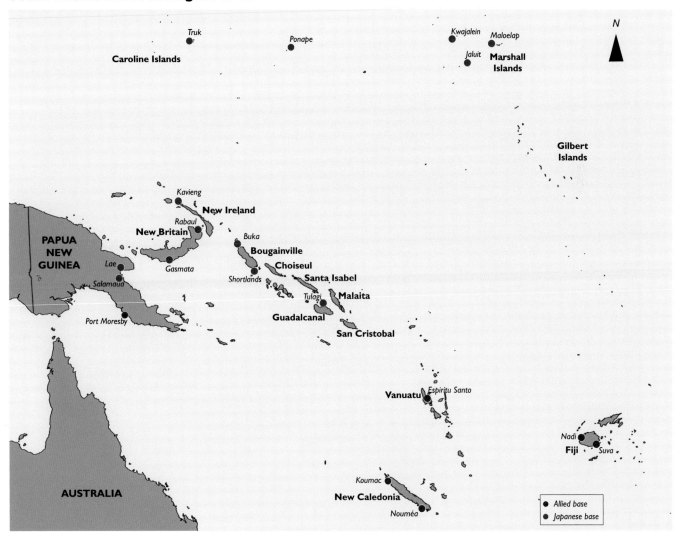

On 30 June, the light cruisers *Tenryū* and *Tatsuta*, part of Sentai 18, left the anchorage at Truk in the Caroline Islands and headed for Guadalcanal, escorting the 13th Airfield Construction Unit. They arrived on 6 July, shortly after the Allied reconnaissance plane had alerted Nimitz of their plans. The engineers landed without incident and began turning open ground into a runway suitable for large aircraft. Both cruisers departed for the large IJN base at Rabaul.

Rabaul was the southern bastion of the Japanese Empire. Originally a seat of the German colonial government of New Guinea, Rabaul was seized by Australian forces during World War I. In January 1942, the Japanese occupied the port at the eastern end of New Britain and began turning it into a fortress. The natural harbor provided a strategic anchorage; numerous airfields supported dozens of planes; miles of tunnels gave shelter from aerial attack; and thousands of troops secured the position.

On 14 July 1942, Rabaul became the headquarters of the IJN's newly created Eighth Fleet, led by Vice Admiral Gunichi Mikawa. The Eighth Fleet initially was expected to be the occupying force for Fiji and New Caledonia; after the FS Operation was postponed,

Mikawa was ordered to focus on the defense of the Bismarck Archipelago, Papua New Guinea, and the Solomon Islands. He flew his flag in the heavy cruiser *Chōkai*, and as August approached, Mikawa kept a close eye on offensive operations in Papua New Guinea. Japanese troops had landed at Buna and Gona on 21 July; they were expected to cross the Owen Stanley Mountains and seize Port Moresby.

LANDINGS ON GUADALCANAL AND TULAGI

Before dawn on 7 August, Admiral Turner's amphibious assault force entered Savo Sound. It divided into two groups. The southern force moved toward Lunga Point; the northern force approached the sheltered anchorage at Tulagi. Shortly after 0600, the assault began with the heavy cruiser *Quincy* (CA-39) and other escorts opening fire on Japanese positions. Planes from the *Saratoga* and *Enterprise* struck targets ashore. By 0900, the first waves of the assault force were on their way from landing zone "X-Ray" toward "Red Beach" between the Tenaru River and Koli Point. Japanese opposition was practically nonexistent. The "defenders" of Guadalcanal were primarily laborers, and they withdrew to the

RearAdmiral Richmond Kelly Turner and Major General Alexander A. Vandegrift confer on the flag bridge of the attack transport *McCawley* (APA-4) in preparation for the landings on Guadalcanal. (National Archives)

The island of Tanambogo burns. Photographed from an SBD Dauntless on 7 August 1942. The view looks east-southeast. Gavutu is to the right of the smoke; the causeway separating the two islands can be seen under the darkest cloud. Florida Island is in the distance. (National Archives)

village of Kukum. The attackers seized the airfield by midafternoon, along with vital machinery and supplies. By nightfall, 11,000 Marines were ashore.

Across the sound, the situation was very different. The Japanese defenders, members of the Kure 3rd Special Naval Landing Force (*rikusentai*), had seized Tulagi in May and dug defensive positions on Tulagi and the smaller twin islands of Gavutu and Tanambogo. The 1st Marine Raider Battalion, under Colonel Merritt A. Edson, landed on Tulagi's "Blue Beach" starting at 0800. They crossed to the eastern shore of the island and then advanced southeast. The defenders notified Mikawa of the assault, indicating that "enemy strength is overwhelming." They resolved to defend to the last man. The Raiders, assisted by naval bombardment and aerial attacks, gradually pushed the defenders back. By dusk only Hill 281, which dominated the southern tip of the island, remained in Japanese hands. The *rikusentai* sniped at the Marines and attempted to infiltrate their positions throughout the night, but Edson and his men secured the island early the next morning.

In the meantime, the 1st Marine Parachute Battalion, commanded by Major Robert H. Williams, was struggling to secure Gavutu and Tanambogo. Its assault began with a landing on Gavutu at noon. Opposition was fierce. Each island was dominated by a single hill, and fire from the Japanese entrenchments on either of them could cover both islands. When Williams's men landed, they were caught in a crossfire, suffering 10 percent casualties within the first two hours. Williams himself was seriously injured leading an assault on Gavutu's Hill 148. It was 1800 before a determined effort seized the summit, but the Japanese on Tanambogo held on. Efforts to storm the narrow causeway joining the two islands were pushed back. A nocturnal landing attempt was thwarted after a shell from a supporting destroyer set fire to a fuel dump, illuminating the landing boats and subjecting them to accurate Japanese fire. Just before noon on 8 August, the 3rd Battalion of the 2d Marine Regiment landed on Gavutu. It brought two light tanks and lighters to ferry them to Tanambogo. Their amphibious assault took place after 1600 that afternoon. One tank outran its supporting Marines and was knocked out. The other methodically overwhelmed Japanese positions; by 2200, both islands were secured. General Vandegrift remarked on the stubbornness of the defense, noting that each Japanese "fought until he was killed."

Word of the assault on Guadalcanal and Tulagi quickly reached the Japanese high command. Admiral Matome Ugaki, Chief of Staff to Admiral Yamamoto, recorded the sense of urgency in his diary:

> This enemy employed a huge force, intending to capture that area once and for all. That we failed to discover it until attacked deserves censure as extremely careless. A warning had been issued two days before. Anyway, we were attacked unprepared. Unless we destroy them promptly, they will attempt to recapture Rabaul, not to speak of frustrating our Moresby operation. Our operations in that area will become extremely unfavorable. We should, therefore, make every effort to drive the enemy down first, even by putting off the Indian Ocean operation. We have made necessary arrangements accordingly.

—7 AUGUST 1942, FROM *FADING VICTORY: THE DIARY OF ADMIRAL MATOME UGAKI, 1941–1945* (NAVAL INSTITUTE PRESS, 1991)

Rear Admiral Sadayoshi Yamada, commander of the 5th Air Attack Force, was responsible for IJN aerial operations in the southern theater. His planes operated from Rabaul, Lae in Papua, and (until that morning) Tulagi. Upon receiving word of the invasion, Yamada reacted immediately. He dispatched a strike of 27 Mitsubishi G4M Type 1 land attack planes (called "Bettys" by the Allies) escorted by 18 Mitsubishi A6M Type 0 fighters (famous Zeros, nicknamed "Zekes" by the Allies). The Betty bombers had been armed for an attack on an Allied airfield in New Guinea, and Yamada rushed them into the air without rearming them, so they attacked with high explosive bombs instead of torpedoes. The escorting Zeros battled the combat air patrol guarding Turner's

Guadalcanal and Surrounding Islands

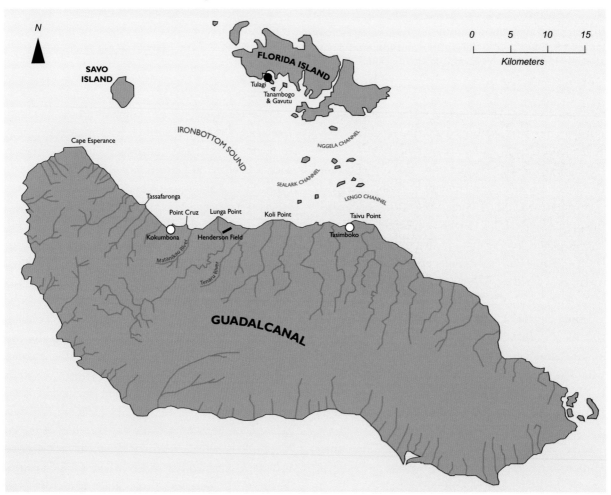

A Marine Corps light tank (M2A4 Stuart) is hoisted from the transport *Alchiba* (AKA-6) into a landing craft on the first day of the Guadalcanal landings. Tanks such as this one helped overcome Japanese resistance on Gavutu. (National Archives)

Wreckage from a Japanese "Betty" land attack plane floats on the surface, 8 August 1942. This was one of 17 lost in the major strike that day. Photographed from the destroyer *Ellet*. (National Archives)

assault force while the Bettys attacked. None of them managed to score any hits, but nine Grumman F4F Wildcat fighters were lost.

Yamada followed up this strike with an even more desperate mission. He sent nine Aichi D3A Type 99 carrier bombers ("Vals" to the Allies) on a one-way strike against the invasion forces. They lacked the range to fly 560 miles from Rabaul, make their attacks, and then return, so they were instructed to ditch their planes in the sheltered waters of the Shortland Islands on the southern tip of Bougainville. Three bombers focused on the destroyer *Mugford* (DD-389). One bomb killed 22 men and wrecked the after deckhouse. Another bomb nearly missed. The other six Vals went after the transports, but before they could get into attack position, the Wildcats began to close. The attackers dove on the destroyer *Dewey* (DD-349) instead but failed to score any hits. Just four of them survived to ditch in the Shortlands.

Yamada hoped to achieve more the following day. At 0800 on 8 August, he sent 26 torpedo-armed Bettys and 15 Zeros to Guadalcanal. They were sighted by Lieutenant W. J. "Jack" Read, a "coastwatcher" of the Royal Australian Naval Volunteer Reserve hiding in the jungles of northern Bougainville. His report reached Turner within an hour, so, when the bombers appeared off the eastern tip of Florida Island, the ships were prepared. The Bettys approached at low altitude, initially heading for the transport group off Tulagi, but they turned to go after those near Guadalcanal. The long, low-altitude run across the sound drew accurate fire from Turner's escorting vessels and patrolling fighters. One damaged bomber crashed into the rear deck of the transport *George F. Elliott* (AP-13); another successfully torpedoed the destroyer *Jarvis* (DD-393). Seventeen of the attacking Bettys were lost and another crash landed; a total of 125 bomber crewmen, including all of the officers, were lost in the attack. It was the heaviest single loss of Japanese land-attack aircraft during the entire campaign.

Three of the 26 Japanese "Betty" land attack planes that struck on 8 August 1942. Note how close they are to the surface of the sea as they make their attack runs. (National Archives)

A few surviving bombers flew over friendly ships on their way back to Rabaul. Vice Admiral Mikawa was leading a strike force of seven cruisers and one destroyer through the waters off Choiseul Island toward the invasion forces. Upon hearing of the Allied assault on 7 August, he immediately resolved to attack with his available forces. Five heavy cruisers had just departed Kavieng, on the northern coast of New Ireland. The *Chōkai* was one of them. The others were the four ships of Cruiser Division 6: the *Aoba, Kako, Kinugasa,* and *Furutaka.* Mikawa summoned them all to Rabaul. The *Chōkai* and destroyer *Yunagi* entered the harbor while the others waited in the waters outside. That afternoon, Mikawa boarded the *Chōkai* and led his formation, now augmented by the light cruisers *Tenryū* and *Yubari,* toward Guadalcanal. He would command them in the campaign's first night action—the Battle of Savo Island—just after midnight on 9 August.

THE BATTLE OF SAVO ISLAND

Rear Admiral V. A. C. Crutchley of the Royal Navy, seconded at the time to the Royal Australian Navy (RAN), commanded Turner's screen. He arranged his forces so that they covered each of the three main entrances to the sound. To the east, guarding the channels that separated Florida Island and Guadalcanal, Crutchley positioned Rear Admiral Norman Scott with the light cruisers USS *San Juan* (CL-54) and HMAS *Hobart* and two destroyers. South of Savo, between that island and the northern coast of Guadalcanal, he placed his flagship, the cruiser HMAS *Australia,* the cruisers HMAS *Canberra* and USS *Chicago* (CA-29), and the U.S. destroyers *Patterson* (DD-392) and *Bagley* (DD-386). Father north, guarding the gap between Florida Island and Savo, Captain Frederick Riefkohl, on board the cruiser USS *Vincennes* (CA-44), led a U.S. formation with the cruisers *Quincy* and *Astoria* (CA-34), escorted by the destroyers *Wilson* (DD-408) and *Helm*

The island of Tulagi provided a sheltered anchorage for the repair of damaged ships and a base for PT boats and other small combatants. This picture is from 1943, after the campaign for Guadalcanal had been brought to a successful conclusion. (National Archives)

One of the last photographs of the cruiser *Astoria*. She is approaching the Guadalcanal invasion beaches on 6 August 1942. (National Archives)

A beautiful color photograph of the heavy cruiser *Quincy*, taken from the aircraft carrier *Wasp* at Nouméa, New Caledonia, on 3 August 1942, before the task force departed for the invasion of Guadalcanal. Note the Measure 12 (modified) camouflage scheme. (National Archives)

(DD-388). These arrangements were designed to counter the threat of submarines; Crutchley had fought German U-boats in the Atlantic and considered Japanese submarines the greatest nocturnal threat. Each mixed cruiser-destroyer formation was arranged so that the destroyers acted as an antisubmarine screen for the cruisers.

Both Crutchley and Turner assumed they would receive adequate warning of an approaching enemy surface force, either from reconnaissance aircraft or from two radar picket destroyers, the *Blue* (DD-387) and *Ralph Talbot* (DD-390), stationed about five miles beyond the western entrances to the sound. The aerial reconnaissance worked as expected; at about 1900 on the evening of 8 August, Turner received word that an enemy force of three cruisers, two destroyers, and two seaplane tenders or gunboats had been sighted northeast of Bougainville at 1025 that morning by an Australian patrol plane. This was Mikawa's force; the erroneous inclusion of "seaplane tenders" in the sighting report led Turner to conclude that the Japanese were going to establish a seaplane base at Rekata Bay on the north coast of

The Loss of the *Quincy*

Just before Plot reported ready to control forward, the ship was hit in the 1.1-in mounts on the main deck aft which was immediately followed by a nine-gun salvo from the *Quincy*'s turrets. The spot on this salvo was down 200, no change. The fire was opened with an estimated range of 6000 yards, target angle of 60 degrees, and a speed believed to be 15 knots. Just before the first salvo was fired a radar range of 5800 yards was obtained. The bearing was drawing rapidly aft on the port side, and when Director 1 reported that they could no longer bear, control was shifted to Director 2 in order to fire Turret 3. At this point, Turret 3 reported being hit and jammed in train. Word was then received in Control Forward from the

Bridge that the ship was changing course to starboard. In the meantime, the plane on the port catapult was lighted off by a hit, apparently an over from a salvo fired at the adjacent cruiser. From this time on the ship was repeatedly hit by large and small caliber shells throughout her full length as she was turning. Control was shifted back to Director 1 and it was trained out to starboard to pick up the enemy as the ship swung around. Turrets 1 and 2 followed in train. The starboard AA battery was ordered to illuminate with star shells as soon as the battery would bear. Three salvoes were fired by this battery before it was put out of action. Two salvoes were fired by Turrets 1 and 2 to starboard before Turret 2 exploded and was burned in some manner and Turret 1 out of action. No men are known to have escaped from Turret 2. At this time, all communication was lost with all stations by Control Forward by any means whatsoever—SS telephones, primary telephones, or auxiliary telephones. . . .

In the meantime, the Bridge had been hit, killing practically everyone in the Pilot House; Battle 2, killing nearly all there; the forward and after 20-mm clipping rooms were hit, and burnt out; boats on the boat deck set on fire; and the 5-in battery and searchlights . . . on both sides and most of the ready boxes either exploded or burnt out. Radio 1 was struck and filled with shrapnel, both stacks perforated, the galley on fire, the hangar and well deck a blazing inferno, the steam escaping from Number 1 stack was deafening, and Battle 2 in flames. The forward Battle Lookout Station was hit as was also the 1.1-in clipping room which was burnt out, the flames enveloping the Forward Control Station and reaching up to the Forward Sky Director. No water was available topside to fight the fires except on after part of the main deck aft where it was turned on and used to fight the fire in the 1.1-in as long as pressure lasted. During this period an enemy ship with mushroom top stacks was observed passing to port, distance about 2000 yards, shooting with everything she had at the *Quincy*. . . .

By this time the ship was no longer being fired on, was listing rapidly to port, the forecastle was awash, water was coming over the gun deck to port and fires were blazing intermittently throughout the whole length of the ship. The party from aloft found nothing but carnage about the gun decks and dense smoke and heat coming from below decks, the ship nearly dead in the water and listing rapidly to port. They assisted in cutting away life rafts, life nets, breaking out life preservers and throwing overboard floatable objects and were ordered to abandon ship by the senior officer present in the vicinity—the gunnery officer—as the water at this point was nearly all the way across the gun deck. About a minute later, the ship capsized to port, the bow went under, the stern raised, and the ship slid from view into the depths.

—LIEUTENANT COMMANDER HARRY B. HENEBERGER, SENIOR SURVIVING OFFICER, USS *QUINCY*

Santa Isabel. From there, they could deliver more frequent strikes on his ships. Distracted by this threat and fatigued by the strenuous operations of the past two days, Turner and Crutchley failed to anticipate a night surface action.

The radar pickets failed to detect Mikawa and his ships. The *Blue* and *Ralph Talbot* were equipped with SC search radars, which could detect approaching surface ships at distances between four and ten miles. However, the littoral conditions in the narrow waters around Guadalcanal reflected the radar waves and made it difficult to interpret return signals. As Mikawa's ships approached the entrance south of Savo Island, they passed within about 10,000 yards of the *Blue*. Her radar operators and lookouts never noticed the Japanese ships. Anxious lookouts on board the *Chōkai* and *Aoba* watched the destroyer steaming away from them as she continued her patrol.

Crutchley did not anticipate this failure. After the battle, he commented, "It should not have been possible for an enemy force to get inside Savo Island without being detected . . . by *Blue* or *Ralph Talbot*." Unaware of the approaching danger, Crutchley was in conference with Turner when Mikawa's force entered the sound at 26 knots. Crutchley took the *Australia* with him to Turner's flagship, so when the Japanese attacked the southern cruiser group, the Allied ships were seriously outgunned. They were also taken completely by surprise; all the commanding officers, except Commander Frank Walker of the *Patterson*, were asleep, exhausted from the intensive operations over the past two days.

Mikawa fired torpedoes first. Sailors on board the *Canberra* noted them passing down either side of the ship as the *Chōkai* opened fire. A seaplane, launched earlier from one of Mikawa's cruisers, dropped flares over the transports, backlighting the *Chicago* and *Canberra* as the Japanese engaged. Within five minutes, the *Canberra* had been hit by at least 24 shells. Her commanding officer, Captain H. B. Farncomb, RAN, was mortally wounded, and her gunnery officer was killed. Hits knocked out all power and opened holes in the side of the ship, causing a gradual list to port that eventually reached 30 degrees. The *Chicago* was hit by two torpedoes. One blew off a small portion of her bow; the other hit amidships but failed to detonate. A shell landed against her foremast, showering the topside with fragments. Her commanding officer, Captain Howard D. Bode, maneuvered to avoid torpedo wakes and chased ghosts to the west, taking the *Chicago* out of the fight.

The *Chōkai* displays the graceful lines typical of IJN cruisers. Note her seaplane amidships, the large bridge structure, and the shade obscuring her foremost turret. Her torpedo ports amidships are closed, but the outlines of the openings can be discerned. The *Chōkai* used her torpedoes and guns very effectively at Savo Island. (U.S. Naval Institute Photo Archive)

The *Quincy*, photographed from a Japanese cruiser, burns while illuminated by searchlights. This photograph was taken shortly before the U.S. cruiser went down. (Naval History and Heritage Command)

Mikawa sighted Riefkohl's cruisers to the northeast around a heavy bank of clouds and turned his ships to engage. As they bore down, Commander Walker, who had alertly been warning the screening forces of the danger, transmitted his second contact report. It was received on board the *Quincy* just before the Japanese opened fire, but it never made it to Riefkohl. Mikawa fired torpedoes, and two minutes later turned on brilliant searchlights. The *Chōkai*, *Aoba*, and *Kako* illuminated the three U.S. cruisers, and each selected a target corresponding to their position in line. Opening salvoes were short. Riefkohl, who initially thought he was being engaged by friendly ships, returned fire with determination, but the Japanese found the range first. The *Aoba* and *Kako* hit the *Quincy* and *Vincennes*, respectively. The *Chōkai* hit the *Astoria* soon thereafter. These hits started fires, illuminating the American cruisers; with their targets clearly visible, the Japanese turned off their searchlights and fired deliberately. Mikawa's remaining ships approached from the west, catching Riefkohl's ships in a crossfire.

A torpedo slammed into the *Vincennes*, and she started to lose power, but not before she hit the *Kinugasa* and temporarily disabled her steering. Captain Samuel N. Moore turned the *Quincy* to the northeast and closed with Mikawa's column, telling his fire control officer, Lieutenant Commander Harry B. Heneberger, "We are going through the middle. Give them hell!" Three shells from his cruiser crashed into the *Chōkai*, destroying her flag plot, killing 30 men, and starting a fire that burned all her charts. Soon thereafter, two torpedoes opened the *Quincy*'s after firerooms and central station to the sea.

Within 20 minutes, the *Quincy* went down, taking Captain Moore with her. Fifteen minutes later, the *Vincennes* followed. The *Astoria* was reduced to a flaming wreck by dozens of shell hits. She was slowing but still fighting; Lieutenant Commander W. B. Davidson, the communications officer, climbed into Turret 2 and fired one last salvo, scoring another hit on the *Chōkai*. Mikawa's foray into Ironbottom Sound led to one of the worst defeats in the Navy's history, but he withdrew without attacking the transports. The Combined Fleet Staff took note of his success:

A report from the Eighth Fleet early this morning said that five enemy heavy cruisers were sunk by a sudden night assault. They might have seemed big ones in the darkness of night, but, even so, they were a fair result. Putting them together, we believed that all the warships and half of the transports have been sunk, and the fate of the battle has now been settled. However, according to a search this morning . . . ships were sighted at the Tulagi area in spite of the fog, and there was no sign of their leaving. . . . Unless we launch all-out attacks after today, we have to realize that the enemy attempt cannot be frustrated.

—9 AUGUST 1942, FROM *FADING VICTORY: THE DIARY OF ADMIRAL MATOME UGAKI, 1941–1945* (NAVAL INSTITUTE PRESS, 2008)

The *Astoria* remained afloat until after noon on 9 August, long enough to disembark her survivors. The remaining men on board the *Canberra* were also taken off, and a torpedo from the destroyer *Ellet* (DD-398) sank her that morning. Mikawa did not escape unscathed. The *Chōkai*, *Kinugasa*, and *Aoba* were hit, and on the return voyage, the *Kako* was torpedoed by the submarine USS *S-44*. Explosions tore open the cruiser's hull, and she sank north of New Ireland on the morning of 10 August. Despite this loss, Mikawa had decimated the Allied screening forces. Turner withdrew, leaving General Vandegrift and his Marines in possession of the island and its airfield but unable to contest the waters around Guadalcanal. Mikawa and his ships seized the opportunity to harass the isolated Marine garrison and land reinforcements. As Ghormley noted in his action report, "The success or failure of this operation cannot yet be judged, as it depends on our ability to hold what we have taken." The Navy would spend the rest of the year attempting to hold Guadalcanal.

The last moments of the cruiser HMAS *Canberra*, listing and burning at about 0630 on 9 August. The destroyer *Blue* is alongside her port bow, removing survivors. The destroyer *Patterson* approaches from astern. Within less than two hours, the *Canberra* would be scuttled by torpedo from the destroyer *Ellet*. (National Archives)

SHIPS, TACTICS, AND TECHNOLOGY

A forward view of the destroyer USS *Aaron Ward*, while in New York on 15 May 1942. Note her main armament of 5-inch/38-caliber guns, the Mk. 37 gun director with FD (Mk. 4) radar, and her camouflage scheme. The cylinders on the port side are 5-inch powder cannisters. (National Archives)

The fight for Guadalcanal was a clash of prewar navies. In the eight months since Pearl Harbor, neither side had been able to bring significant new forces to bear, and insufficient experience had been gained to revise prewar tactics and doctrine. Guadalcanal would be a crucible that challenged prewar thinking in both navies, exposing weaknesses and critical flaws. Both sides brought different perspectives. For the IJN, night battle was an opportunity to utilize stealth and capitalize on the fighting strength of individual ships. The U.S. Navy, in contrast, saw night action as fundamentally uncertain, a gamble that was best avoided. These perspectives, and the assumptions embedded within them, had a significant influence on the outcome of the battles off Guadalcanal.

U.S. NAVY TACTICS AND DOCTRINE

During the interwar period (1919–1939), the Navy prepared for a transoceanic campaign in the Pacific against Japan. The Navy assumed that the battle fleet would move across the Pacific, seize advanced bases, defeat the IJN in a decisive battle, and ultimately blockade the Japanese Home Islands. Interwar exercises explored how to best to accomplish this; they investigated how to coordinate the movements of the fleet and its supporting forces—transports, supply vessels, and repair ships—over great distances. The annual fleet training regimen supported and helped refine the planning process; it was a yearly cycle that began by integrating new sailors into the fleet and culminated with a "Fleet Problem." Twenty-one Fleet Problems were held between 1923 and 1940. These large exercises pitted one part of the fleet against another in mock combat. They also investigated the challenges of a trans-Pacific campaign.

There were many challenges. The distances were extreme. A successful campaign required moving the fleet from the base at Pearl Harbor, through the Marshall and Caroline island groups—called the Japanese "Mandates" because Japan was mandated dominion over them by the Treaty of Versailles—and into the western Pacific, some 5,000 miles. Once there, the fleet would seize a base and impose a strangling blockade on Japan; gradual pressure was expected to force Japan's rulers to submit, but at some point, the IJN would contest these operations and seek battle with its main fleet. To maximize the chances of victory, the IJN was expected to subject the U.S. fleet to attritional attacks, reducing its strength. The main action would most likely come when the Navy's forces were at their weakest.

The campaign plan had important implications for the Navy's tactics and doctrine. Even though the Navy would be on the strategic offensive, the IJN was expected to have the tactical initiative. They would choose the time and place of the major battles that would decide the campaign. This led to an emphasis on concentration. The battle fleet had to be kept together; otherwise, the Japanese would strike when it was dispersed and defeat it in detail. Tactical exercises and the Fleet Problems reflected this assumption and stressed the importance of concentration.

The Fleet Problems and tactical exercises reflected another important assumption: the Navy's belief that battle was inherently uncertain. Success or failure could not be predicted; it was heavily dependent on the skill and expertise of officers at all levels, from the fleet commander down. The Navy sought to capitalize on this by using "mission" orders that framed the context for subordinates, gave them an objective, and allowed them to flexibly meet it. Officers practiced writing these orders and carrying them out in regular exercises. The approach helped foster the creativity of individual commanders. Since each situation had to be assessed on its own merits, exercises challenged commanders to come up with creative approaches that would win victory; the contested nature of the exercises—officers fought against each other on opposing sides—motivated them to formulate new tactics. Officers continually refined and enhanced the Navy's tactical doctrines during the interwar period.

Three dominant approaches emerged and became the basis of the service's tactics. The first was the assumption that the best way to achieve victory in a naval battle was to seize the initiative and control the battle's tempo. Even if the IJN initiated the action, the Navy expected to be able to use maneuver and well-timed attacks to knock the Japanese off balance and take control. Officers were conditioned in peacetime exercises to act aggressively and seize the initiative. One of the best ways to do this was by opening fire at the earliest possible moment; accordingly, the second dominant approach was an emphasis on the importance of gunfire in a surface action. Navy ships practiced opening fire as soon as a target was sighted in the hope of gaining an initial advantage. The last dominant approach sought to capitalize on the momentary

OFFICIAL PHOTOGRAPH
NOT TO BE RELEASED
FOR PUBLICATION
NAVY YARD MARE ISLAND, CALIF.

RESTRICTED

3555-42   U.S.S. HELENA (CL50)
PLAN VIEW AMIDSHIPS
MARE ISLAND, CAL.   JUNE 27, 1942

The light cruiser *Helena* at the Mare Island Navy Yard in California, 27 June 1942. Her forward superstructure had been reconfigured to include an open bridge and smaller lower bridge wings. Her fore Mk. 34 main battery gun director, with a FC (Mk. 3) fire control radar, is immediately in front of the foremast. The other director, just behind the open bridge, is a Mk. 33, with a FD (Mk. 4) radar mounted on its front. (National Archives)

difficult to assess their effectiveness, but there was no doubt that destroyers posed a serious threat to larger vessels, including battleships. The IJN was expected to make similar attacks, and so the Navy explored how best to protect the battle fleet at night. Over the course of the interwar period, these exercises began to increasingly emphasize the importance of gunfire. A new model for night surface action emerged. Instead of stealthily approaching their targets, destroyers began to fight their way to attack position with guns blazing. By the time they got within torpedo range, surprise would be lost. Destroyer commanders became adept at using their guns and firing torpedoes, but aggressive gunfire became more important than remaining hidden. This prewar training would have serious ramifications for the fighting off Guadalcanal.

U.S. NAVY RADAR

The U.S. Navy's willingness to explore new approaches led it to rapidly embrace new technologies. Radar was one of the most important. Experimental radars were installed in ships before the war, and, by the time of the attack on Pearl Harbor, the Navy was starting to integrate radar with fleet operations. Radar came in two basic varieties, each developed under the cognizance of a different technical bureau. Search radars were the responsibility of the Bureau of Ships; fire control radars were developed by the Bureau of Ordnance.

The SC was the Navy's primary search radar in 1942. Under the right conditions, it was capable of detecting large surface ships at 10 miles and aircraft at 30. However, its effectiveness was limited by the A-Scope display, a modified oscilloscope that showed the strength of a return signal on its vertical axis and range on the horizontal. To identify a target, an operator would pause the radar's rotation to get an accurate "fix" on the range and bearing. SC radars with A-Scopes could search for targets or "fix" existing ones; they

opportunities that would appear in battle. The Navy planned to leverage the flexibility and initiative of individual officers by emphasizing decentralized control; each officer would work toward a general plan but was expected to act on his own initiative. Together, these three ideas gave the Navy a powerful framework for coordinating action in battle.

However, they also prevented the Navy from exploring alternatives. The emphasis on gunfire limited the Navy's ability to attack effectively with torpedoes. At the start of the interwar period, destroyer tactics emphasized stealthy attacks under cover of darkness; destroyers would attempt to approach their targets unseen, fire their torpedoes, and get away. The artificialities involved in these mock attacks made it

could not do both simultaneously. The SG radar, the Navy's first microwave radar, addressed this problem. It introduced a new display, the Plan-Position-Indicator (PPI), that presented a top-down "bird's eye" view of the surrounding area with the radar at the center, allowing search and target tracking to occur simultaneously. It also could detect surface ships at greater distances, more than 20 miles for a battleship. Very few ships that fought at Guadalcanal were equipped with the SG, but those that had it consistently developed a better view of the situation around them.

Fire control radars leveraged the same technology but operated differently. The FC (Mk. 3) and FD (Mk. 4) were designed to provide greater directional accuracy, so that they could track a target precisely, both in range and bearing. The FC was intended for surface fire and equipped the main batteries of battleships

The forward superstructure of the battleship *Washington*, photographed at the New York Navy Yard on 18 August 1942. Four of her radars are visible. At the very top is an SC search set, below that is an FC radar, atop her main battery Mk. 38 director. Next is the small SG, in front of the fire control tower, and finally an FD, on top of the Mk. 37 secondary battery director. (National Archives)

Navy radar displays

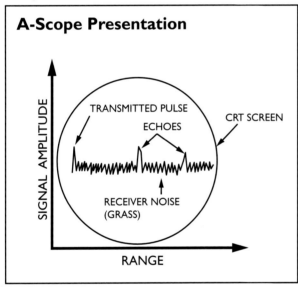

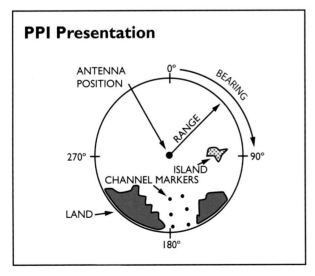

Practicing for Quick and Effective Gunfire on Board the Destroyer *Sterett*

The 5-in loading crews became increasingly competitive during these weeks in the vicinity of Guadalcanal. One morning Chief [Gunner's Mate Hiram] Hodge asked me to officiate at a loading contest between the crews of guns Number 2 and Number 4. The contest was to measure stamina as well as speed. Each crew would load four hundred rounds; the winner would be the one that completed the task in the shortest time. This race was a matter of intense interest to the entire ship's company, and a considerable sum of money was riding on it—four thousand dollars, to be exact. I became the custodian of the pot and scheduled the contest to begin at 1400.

At the appointed hour, everyone who was not on watch was at the loading machine. The gun captains drew lots, and gun Number 2 picked the leadoff spot. This was Big Willie's crew and as first shellman he

18

was without question the key man on that team. With stopwatch in hand, I shouted, "Go!" Big Willie attacked each shell as it came up in the shell hoist, handling them as if they weighed five pounds instead of fifty-five. His movements were fluid and graceful, and there was no wasted motion. The noise of the loading machine took on a cadence of its own as one after another the shells came out of the hoist, were put in the tray, and went into the breech. Big Willie averaged about four seconds per load at first, and I waited for the pace to slow as he grew tired. But it did not slow. It continued for five, then, even twenty minutes, and within thirty minutes the crew of gun Number 2 had loaded four hundred rounds. Big Willie and his teammates looked as fresh as when they had started.

Now came Jim Grann's turn. He was younger and an inch or two taller than Big Willie, but not quite as muscular. He started out like a sprinter. Again the shells landed in the tray with a regular cadence. But after twenty minutes the pace slowed, and after thirty minutes (still short of the four hundred rounds) Grann was very tired and had trouble moving the shells. Gun Number 2 had won, hands down. I presented the four thousand dollars to Big Willie for distribution to his mates and congratulated both crews. This performance assured us all that when our time came to fight, we would acquit ourselves well.

—C. RAYMOND CALHOUN, *TIN CAN SAILOR: LIFE ABOARD THE USS* STERETT, *1939–1945* (NAVAL INSTITUTE PRESS, 1993, 2000)

and cruisers. The FD applied the same technology in three dimensions so that it could track aircraft as well as surface targets; it was used in destroyers and the secondary batteries of battleships and some cruisers. Operators of both radars used the A-Scope, but the displays were modified so that they could "zoom in" and get higher resolutions of a narrow range band around the target, either 500 or 1,000 yards. In theory, both the FC and FD could be used to fire "blind," with the target obscured by darkness or smoke, but in practice, they lacked sufficient accuracy to do so. Radar ranges had to be combined with visual bearings to score hits.

IMPERIAL JAPANESE NAVY TACTICS AND DOCTRINE

IJN tactics and doctrine were also shaped by the belief that a war was coming in the Pacific. The high-level assumptions of IJN admirals and U.S. Navy officers were largely the same, but their views differed in important details. Both believed the war's centerpiece would be a U.S. strategic offensive, but while the Navy expected the war to be won by a sustained campaign, the IJN assumed a single decisive battle would decide the outcome. Accordingly, IJN officers focused their attention on a major fleet action that they expected to win the war.

The IJN's history had been dominated by decisive battles. It had triumphed over the Chinese at the Battle of the Yalu River in September 1894, winning command of the Yellow Sea and facilitating occupation of the Korean Peninsula and Formosa. In May 1905, at the Battle of Tsushima, the IJN defeated the Russian Baltic Fleet, which had sailed some 18,000 miles only to be destroyed in the waters south of the Sea of Japan. The importance of these victories was amplified by the IJN's interpretation of the writings of American naval theorist Alfred Thayer Mahan, so that by the start of the interwar period, Japanese naval officers focused on a singular, decisive naval battle as the key to winning a war against the United States.

Winning such a battle became more problematic because of the naval arms limitation treaties of the interwar period. Starting with the Washington Treaty of 1922, these restricted the size and power of the IJN's battle fleet, limiting it to three battleships (or battle cruisers) for every five possessed by the U.S. Navy. Under the conditions of the London Treaty of 1930, this meant that the IJN was limited to just nine battleships compared to the 15 in the Navy's battle line. At first, these restrictions applied only to battleships and battle cruisers, but the 1930 treaty extended them to cruisers as well. The IJN's representatives successfully argued for a 7:10 ratio for cruisers, but the 3:5 ratio remained in place for battleships.

These limitations meant that the IJN would be unlikely to succeed in a conventional battle. Even though the U.S. Navy was expected to lose strength as it moved across the Pacific—most analyses assumed a loss of 10 percent for each thousand miles—it would still retain sufficient fighting power to defeat the smaller IJN. Japanese officers sought to make up the difference in several ways. They built ships and weapons of higher quality, developed new and asymmetric tactics, invested in new technologies, and aggressively pursued the development of air power as a decisive arm of naval warfare. Each of these efforts had an impact on the fighting for Guadalcanal.

The superstructure of the heavy cruiser *Atago*. Numerous lookout positions (the small turrets on both sides of the structure) are visible, along with her starboard high-angle rangefinder and searchlight control positions. The IJN used powerful telescopes, visibly protruding from the lookout positions, the same way the Navy used radar at night. Often in 1942, the Japanese scopes were superior at detecting approaching ships than U.S. radar. (U.S. Naval Institute Photo Archive)

Characteristics of Ships That Fought at Guadalcanal

U.S. NAVY

Name	Class	Year	Displacement	Speed	Armament	Armor
Washington, BB-56 (Battleship)	*North Carolina*	1941	37,484 tons	28 knots	9 x 16-in/45 20 x 5-in/38	Belt: 12-in Deck: 5.5-in
San Francisco, CA-38 (Heavy Cruiser)	*New Orleans*	1934	10,136 tons	32.7 knots	9 x 8-in/55 8 x 5-in/25	Belt: 5-in Deck: 2.25-in
Helena, CL-50 (Light Cruiser)	*Brooklyn*	1939	9,767 tons	32.5 knots	15 x 6-in/47 8 x 5-in/38	Belt: 5-in Deck: 2-in
Sterett, DD-407 (Destroyer)	*Benham*	1938	1,657 tons	38.5 knots	4 x 5-in/38 16 x 21-in TT	None
O'Bannon, DD-450 (Destroyer)	*Fletcher*	1942	2,325 tons	38 knots	5 x 5-in/38 10 x 21-in TT	None

IMPERIAL JAPANESE NAVY

Name	Class	Year	Displacement	Speed	Armament	Armor
Hiei (Battleship)	*Kongō*	Rebuilt 1940	36,400 tons	30.5 knots	8 x 14-in/45 14 x 6-in/50 8 x 5-in/40	Belt: 8-in Deck: 4.7-in
Chōkai (Heavy Cruiser)	*Takao*	1932	11,350 tons	35.5 knots	10 x 8-in/50 8 x 5-in/40 8 x 24-in TT	Belt: 3.9-in Deck: 1.4-in
Nagara (Light Cruiser)	*Nagara*	1921	5,570 tons	36 knots	7 x 5.5-in/50 8 x 24-in TT	Belt: 2.5-in Deck: 1.25-in
Akatsuki (Destroyer)	*Akatsuki*	1932	1,680 tons	38 knots	6 x 5-in/50 9 x 24-in TT	None
Asagumo (Destroyer)	*Asashio*	1937	1,961 tons	35 knots	6 x 5-in/50 8 x 24-in TT	None

The emphasis on higher quality led to ship designs that packed powerful weaponry into relatively small hulls. This was especially true of cruisers and destroyers. Starting with the *Nachi*-class ships of 1928 and 1929, IJN heavy cruisers were armed with ten 8-inch guns in five twin turrets; their U.S. counterparts typically had nine, in three triple turrets. The contemporary *Fubuki*-class destroyers mounted six 5-inch guns. Most U.S. destroyers from the period had just four. But it was with torpedoes that the IJN revolutionized night combat. The newer Japanese cruisers and destroyers carried the Type 93 torpedo, the "Long Lance." These 24-inch weapons were powered by oxygen, rather than regular air, giving them unprecedented speed and range. The Type 93 could travel farther at its highest speed setting (21,900 yards at 50 knots) than the comparable Navy Mark 15 could at its lowest (15,000 yards at 26.5 knots).

Japanese *Suichūdan* Shells

The Type 88 and Type 91 AP shells were intended primarily as normal AP shells and their *suichū* properties were considered subsidiary, with the aim of increasing the effective hitting area in case of short near misses. In direct hits, the shell functioned as a standard AP shell; in a near miss, the shell could result in an underwater hit, below the [armor] belt, provided it fell within a 100-200-caliber distance from the side and with an optimal falling angle. In that case the "windshield" and the cap-head broke off upon hitting the water, and the now flat-headed shell continued on a stable directory below the surface. In fact, this happened only once during the Pacific War when . . . a Type 91 20-cm No. 2 AP shell fired by the *Kinugasa* hit the *Boise* during the Battle of Cape Esperance.

—ERIC LACROIX AND LINTON WELLS II, *JAPANESE CRUISERS OF THE PACIFIC WAR* (NAVAL INSTITUTE PRESS, 1997)

The IJN developed two specific tactics to harness the capabilities of these torpedoes. At night, before the main battle-line action, cruisers and destroyers, supported by high-speed battleships, would attack the Navy's formation from three directions. One group would attack each bow and a third would attack from the rear. They would destroy any screening vessels and fire their torpedoes from long range into the heart of the U.S. battle line. The attack was expected to cripple the Navy's formation and leave it ripe for defeat in a daylight action the next morning. In the daylight battle, the IJN cruisers and destroyers would advance ahead of the Japanese battle line, flank the American forces, and fire more salvoes of the deadly torpedoes. Combined with the fire of the IJN's battleships, this attack was designed to disrupt the Navy's cohesion and bring victory.

Triumph would be aided by additional technological investments. The Japanese developed a powerful

The heavy cruiser *Chōkai*, flagship of Vice Admiral Mikawa's Eighth Fleet, during a firing exercise in 1938. Like many other IJN heavy cruisers, she was armed with ten 8-inch guns in five twin turrets. She also carried a large battery of 24-inch Type 93 torpedoes. (U.S. Naval Institute Photo Archive)

An amidships view of the newly completed heavy cruiser *Takao*, taken on 20 May 1932. The large ports for her Type 93 torpedoes are visible; the forward mount is trained slightly out. Also visible are lookout positions on her superstructure, two of her high-angle guns, and, on top of the superstructure, her large 4.5-meter rangefinder and main battery director. (U.S. Naval Institute Photo Archive)

naval air arm that integrated carrier- and land-based aircraft into a decisive weapon. The events of December 1941 illustrated its potential. The First Air Fleet—the famous *Kidō Butai*—destroyed the U.S. Navy's battle line in the raid on Pearl Harbor, while land-based attack aircraft— the Mitsubishi G3M ("Nell" in the Allied code) and G4M Betty—sank the Royal Navy's *Prince of Wales* and *Repulse*. The IJN anticipated using these planes, flying from a network of air bases in the Mandates, to cooperate with the First Air Fleet to attack, damage, and seriously attrite the U.S. fleet before the decisive battle. Simultaneously, the IJN's submarine force would attempt to intercept the American forces and attack them with torpedoes. Although the submarine torpedoes were not as large or powerful as the Long Lance, they were still deadly. The potential of the IJN's submarine force was augmented by the use of midget submarines. Although

most famously used in attacks on harbors—such as Pearl Harbor, Sydney, and Diego Suarez—the midget submarines originally were developed to be used as part of the main fleet action; special tenders would bring the midgets to the area and launch them in the path of the Navy's ships.

Finally, toward the end of the decisive battle, the IJN expected to close the range and use special *Suichūdan* (underwater) shells to sink Navy ships. The potential of these shells was discovered by accident in 1924 when a 16-inch shell fired at the incomplete battleship *Tosa* entered the water, traveled a relatively straight path, penetrated the hull below the water line, and exploded in the engineering spaces. The IJN investigated the physics involved and developed armor-piercing (AP) shells designed to give a predictable underwater trajectory and replicate that performance.

Naval Guns

U.S. NAVY

Gun	Projectile Weight	Range	Firing Cycle	Notes
16-in/45	2,700 pounds	36,900 yards	30 seconds	Main battery of *Washington* and *South Dakota*
8-in/55	260 pounds	31,869 yards	18 seconds	Main battery of heavy cruisers
6-in/47	130 pounds	26,118 yards	6–8 seconds	Main battery of *Helena* and *Boise*
5-in/38	55 pounds	18,200 yards	3 seconds	Main battery of *Atlanta*, *Juneau*, and destroyers. Secondary battery of other ships.

IMPERIAL JAPANESE NAVY

Gun	Projectile Weight	Range	Firing Cycle	Notes
14-in/45	1,485 pounds	38,770 yards	30 seconds	Main battery of *Hiei* and *Kirishima*
8-in/50	277.45 pounds	31,600 yards	15 seconds	Main battery of heavy cruisers
6-in/50	100 pounds	22,970 yards	10 seconds	Secondary battery of *Hiei* and *Kirishima*
5.5-in/50	83.8 pounds	21,600 yards	10 seconds	Main battery of light cruisers
5-in/50	50.7 pounds	20,100 yards	6–12 seconds	Main battery of destroyers
5-in/40	50.7 pounds	16,075 yards	5–8 seconds	Secondary battery of later heavy cruisers
5-in/40	45 pounds	17,500 yards	6 seconds	Secondary battery of *Chōkai*, *Kako*-class, and *Aoba*-class heavy cruisers

Torpedo Comparison

Description	Range	Weight	Warhead	Notes
Japanese Type 93 (24-in)	21,900 yards at 50 knots 35,000 yards at 42 knots 43,700 yards at 38 knots	5952 pounds	1080 pounds Type 97 (60% TNT, 40% HND)	Oxygen propelled
American Mark 15 (21-in)	6000 yards at 45 knots 10,000 yards at 33.5 knots 15,000 yards at 26.5 knots	3841 pounds	825 pounds TNT	Magnetic as well as contact exploder

THE CAMPAIGN'S FIRST WEEKS

AFTER THEIR VICTORY AT SAVO ISLAND, THE JAPANESE QUICKLY MOVED TO
retake Guadalcanal. Responsibility for the effort fell to Lieutenant General
Harukichi Hyakutake, commander of the 17th Army, with headquarters at
Rabaul. He was overseeing the ongoing offensive in New Guinea and resolved
to rapidly overwhelm the American garrison on Guadalcanal so that the effort
would not drain forces from the campaign to seize Port Moresby. Optimism and
inadequate intelligence led Hyakutake to underestimate General Vandegrift's
numbers. Hyakutake assumed a small offensive would be able retake the
island. Admiral Ugaki's assessment was similar. He expected soon to resume
the offensive.

The most urgent thing at present is to send a troop
there [to Guadalcanal] to mop up the enemy rem-
nant, rescue the garrison, and repair the airfield.
The support force should simultaneously carry out
operations as scheduled while invasions of Moresby,
Ocean, and Nauru islands should be completed as
well as attempting to reduce the enemy strength. I
instructed the staff along these lines.

— 13 AUGUST 1942, FROM *FADING VICTORY: THE DIARY OF ADMIRAL MATOME
UGAKI, 1941–1945* (NAVAL INSTITUTE PRESS, 2008)

Colonel Kiyoano Ichiki was selected to lead the assault. His 28th Infantry Regiment was available since
its original mission—the occupation of Midway—was
no longer feasible. The IJN offered up a contingent of
the well-trained Yokosuka 5th Special Naval Landing
Force to augment Ichiki's attack.

Rear Admiral Raizō Tanaka, commander of
Destroyer Squadron 2 at Rabaul, ferried these forces to
Guadalcanal. He planned to approach at high speed
under the cover of darkness to avoid aerial attack. On
the night of 17 August, he tested his concept by bringing
500 members of the 5th Special Naval Landing Force to
the island and landing them near Kokumbona Village,
west of the Marine perimeter. On the afternoon of 18
August, 916 of Colonel Ichiki's men left their heavy
weapons behind and boarded Tanaka's six destroyers.
They disembarked in the vicinity of Taivu Point, east
of Vandegrift's men. The landings were uneventful;
there were no U.S. forces to oppose this early foray of
the Tokyo Express. On their way out, the destroyers
bombarded the airfield and the docks at Tulagi. Little
damage was done, but the delay allowed B-17 Flying
Fortresses from Espiritu Santo to catch Tanaka the next
day. One bomb damaged the *Hagikaze*. Ichiki gathered
his men and formed up for an assault.

His small force—less than 1,500 men—was expected
to gather up the remnants of the Japanese forces on
the island, integrate them into a combat force, and
overwhelm the Marine garrison, estimated as just 2,000
men. In fact, Vandegrift had 17,000 men defending the
island and the anchorage at Tulagi. Ichiki was infected
with confidence; although the remaining men of his
regiment were scheduled to arrive on the island within
five days, he took the offensive immediately.

Vandegrift did not wait passively for Japanese assaults. He regularly sent patrols beyond his perimeter to probe Japanese positions and disrupt their plans. The day after Ichiki landed, a reconnaissance in force by three companies of the 5th Marine Regiment overwhelmed the Japanese defenders of Kokumbona and Matanikau villages, destroying the offensive potential of the Japanese forces there. Another patrol, led by Captain Charles Brush, struck out eastward on the 19th and ran into a column of Ichiki's men. Brush set up an ambush, killing nearly all the Japanese and gathering valuable intelligence. Vandegrift soon knew Imperial Japanese Army troops were on the island and planning an assault on his eastern perimeter.

It came on the night of 20 August, as the Ichiki Detachment stormed across the mouth of Alligator Creek and initiated the Battle of the Tenaru River. The Marines had prepared for them, digging in, laying barbed wire, and establishing clear fields of fire. Ichiki's men bravely made a series of *banzai* charges, but their assault collapsed against determined resistance. Although some survived to infiltrate the Marine positions, by dawn, every Japanese who had made it across the creek had been killed. The 1st Batalion, 1st Marines, under command of Lieutenant Colonel L. B. Cresswell, crossed Alligator Creek upstream and swept in behind the remaining Japanese, trapping them in a coconut grove. Surrounded, Ichiki's force was gradually destroyed by Marine firepower. Ichiki committed suicide. Fewer than 150 of his men, left behind as a rear guard at Taivu Point, survived.

THE BATTLE OF THE EASTERN SOLOMONS

The Allied code word for the Marine perimeter at Guadalcanal was "Cactus," and on 20 August the first planes of the "Cactus Air Force" arrived. Nineteen Wildcats and 12 SBD Dauntless dive bombers of Marine squadrons VMF-223 and VMSB-232 flew from the escort carrier *Long Island* (CVE-1), landing at Henderson Field in the late afternoon. On the 22nd, these planes were augmented by P-400 Airacobras of the Army's 67th Fighter Squadron.

The failure of Colonel Ichiki's assault convinced Japanese commanders that a more determined effort was necessary. Plans to deliver the remaining men of the 28th Infantry Regiment and the Yokosuka 5th Special Naval Landing Force grew into a complex effort to suppress U.S. forces, seize Guadalcanal, and draw out the remaining American carriers. Admiral Yamamoto hoped he could regain the initiative and make up for the defeat at Midway with a triumph in the Solomons. Vice Admiral Nobutake Kondō led Yamamoto's supporting arm, which included the large carriers *Shōkaku* and *Zuikaku* under the command

Vice Admiral Chūichi Nagumo commanded the Japanese carrier strike force at the battles of the Eastern Solomons and the Santa Cruz Islands. He also commanded the Japanese carriers during the raid on Pearl Harbor and the Battle of Midway. (National Archives)

of Vice Admiral Chūichi Nagumo. Ahead of Nagumo steamed Kondō's advance force and the vanguard group, commanded by Rear Admiral Hiroaki Abe. Abe had the battleships *Hiei* and *Kirishima*. Rear Admiral Tanaka led the transport unit, with 1,500 troops on board the *Kinryu Maru* and four patrol boats.

Although the Japanese had changed their naval code on 13 August, Allied cryptanalysts had a sense that something was under way. On the evening of 20 August, Ghormley shared details of these estimates in a communication to Fletcher, indicating that although the presence of enemy carriers was not "definitely indicated" it was "highly probable." Ghormley expected Fletcher's powerful Task Force (TF) 61—with the carriers *Saratoga*, *Enterprise*, and *Wasp*—to prevent the Japanese from overwhelming the defenders of Henderson Field. Fletcher spent the 21st covering Guadalcanal. The next day, Ghormley let Fletcher know that the Japanese were expected to "attack in force"

Vice Admiral Frank Jack Fletcher commanded the Navy's carrier task forces at Coral Sea, Midway, and the Eastern Solomons, as well as the invasion forces at Guadalcanal. (National Archives)

between 23 and 26 August. That night, Fletcher moved northwest, paralleling the coast of Malaita, anticipating that Japanese forces would come south from Truk.

On the 23rd, a PBY Catalina flying boat sighted Tanaka's transports east of Bougainville. A B-17 reported additional Japanese ships south of the island. With no enemy carriers in sight, Fletcher sent strikes against these targets, but, because Tanaka reversed course, the planes found nothing. Assuming it was safe to detach the *Wasp* to refuel, Fletcher sent her south later that day. Japanese searches found nothing on the 23rd, but Nagumo detached Rear Admiral Chuichi Hara and the light carrier *Ryūjō*, heavy cruiser *Tone*, and two destroyers so that they could close with Guadalcanal,

The First Night on Edson's Ridge

The nightmare got worse. "At this point," said [Private First Class Joe] Rushton, "people were crawling in all directions, mainly away from the log crossing. It wasn't long before they were overrun by the swarming attackers of the main charge. It was horrible and frightening hearing our small group of overrun Raiders screaming as the bastards bayoneted and hacked them with their Samurai swords." Rushton discovered his assistant

BAR [Browning Automatic Rifle] man, Private First Class Kenneth E. Ritter, sprawled nearby, badly shot in the back by the same spray of pointblank automatic fire that had wounded Rushton. "He was in great pain and shock and asked me not to leave him." Rushton's long night was just beginning.

West of Rushton's drama, along the river, Private First Class [John W.] Mielke and the survivors of Sergeant

Boone's machine-gun squad still manned their outpost. Mielke took advantage of a lull in the fighting to ask [Lawrence] "Pappy" Holdren whether Belleau Wood or the Argonne Forest had been any worse than this wild night. Holdren shook his head ruefully. "No," he told Mielke, "This is the worst situation I've ever been in."

—COLONEL JOSEPH H. ALEXANDER, USMC (RET.), *EDSON'S RAIDERS: THE 1ST MARINE RAIDER BATTALION IN WORLD WAR II* (NAVAL INSTITUTE PRESS, 2010)

suppress the airfield, and cover the approach of Tanaka's force. He was expected to land troops on the 25th. Nagumo's large carriers would provide distant cover and ambush any U.S. forces that attempted to interfere.

On the 24th, the Japanese advanced forces—the *Ryūjō* group, Kondō's force, and Abe's battleships—were sighted. Nagumo's carriers remained just beyond the search arcs. Suspecting there might be more enemy forces nearby, Fletcher ordered a search and attack to the northwest from the carrier *Enterprise*. Almost simultaneously, Hara launched the *Ryūjō*'s air group against Henderson Field. They would have attacked in concert with a strike from Rabaul, but those planes turned back because of bad weather.

The *Ryūjō*'s small strike encountered defending Marine Wildcats and failed to do significant damage. In the meantime, search planes from the *Enterprise* had located the *Ryūjō* and her escorts. They attacked alone or in small groups, failing to hit the carrier. Fletcher followed up with a coordinated strike from the *Saratoga*. As the planes attacked, the *Ryūjō* went into a tight starboard turn to present a more difficult target, but, under the guidance of strike commander Commander Harry D. Felt, the Dauntlesses scored three hits and several near misses, starting fires and opening holes in the *Ryūjō*'s hull. Grumman TBF Avengers made one torpedo hit on the starboard side aft that knocked out the starboard engine room and damaged steering. The *Ryūjō* steamed in circles while the fires burned out of control; Rear Admiral Hara was ultimately forced to scuttle her.

Earlier that day, a search plane from the cruiser *Chikuma* had reported an encounter with U.S. carrier fighters before going down. This gave Nagumo a bearing and likely range to Fletcher's task force. He immediately prepared a strike. While it was taking off, two *Enterprise* Dauntlesses at the end of their search pattern found Kondō's group and then Nagumo's force. They climbed to attack altitude and dove on the *Shōkaku*. The carrier barely maneuvered in time. One bomb exploded on the water 10 meters from the starboard side, killing six crewmen. The plucky Dauntlesses escaped, but poor radio reception prevented their sighting report from reaching Fletcher in full, denying him the opportunity for a follow-up strike. Nagumo launched a second strike immediately.

The Second Night on Edson's Ridge

Seven Japanese destroyers opened fire on the Ridge at 2100, but the battle in the jungle commenced almost immediately after dark. Major [Yukichi] Kokusho's platoons filtered forward stealthily, guiding on the parallel lagoon, looking for the boundary between [Captain John B.] Sweeney's [Baker] Company and [Captain William A.] Stiles' [Dog Company of the 1st Engineering Battalion], searching for ways to encircle the outposts.

Those Raiders who survived being posted in such a thin line in the jungle later questioned Edson's tactics, but it is difficult in retrospect to devise a suitable alternative. Edson's mission was to defend Henderson Field at all costs. He made the hard-nosed decision to risk a portion of his command as outguards to detect and disrupt the Japanese advance. In this regard, Red Mike [Edson] established the line of outposts as Civil War generals employed skirmishers. Their duties were remarkably similar: to provide the main body early warning, then force the approaching enemy into a premature deployment, thus slowing his advance. Modern Marines might call this a "speed bump" mission. As costly and traumatic as the experience proved to be for the outguards, there exists plenty of evidence that their exposed position disrupted Major Kokusho's advance significantly.

The Japanese kicked off their assault with a bright magnesium flare. Major Kokusho drew his sword and led his battalion out of the shadows, the riflemen screaming "*Banzai!*" and "Death to Roosevelt!" The burning flare backlit the Raiders, but they were squatting in their shallow fighting holes, heads bent forward along rifle stocks or sighting down machine-gun barrels. The Japanese attacked into the artificial light, running uphill through the thick grass, bunching up against the barbed wire—a virtual shooting gallery for the Marines. Disciplined cross-fire scissored Kokusho's front ranks. Grenades exploded in the crowded back ranks. On they came, lapping up towards the line of foxholes. Raiders on the crest of the spur picked their onrushing targets carefully, shooting the first man, bayoneting the second. The wave broke, receded back down the bloody slope.

—COLONEL JOSEPH H. ALEXANDER, USMC (RET.), *EDSON'S RAIDERS: THE 1ST MARINE RAIDER BATTALION IN WORLD WAR II* (NAVAL INSTITUTE PRESS, 2010)

Radar warned TF 61 of Nagumo's first strike. Fighters were vectored out to intercept while escorts collected around the carriers *Saratoga* and *Enterprise*. The Japanese Val dive bombers broke into two waves as they approached. The first focused on the *Enterprise*; the second skirted eastward and tried to attack the *Saratoga*, ten miles beyond. The battleship *North Carolina* (BB-55), at the rear of the *Enterprise*'s screen, drew several attackers. As the Wildcats engaged the Japanese fighters, the bombers of the first wave closed in and the *North Carolina* "lit up like a Christmas tree." A semi-AP bomb hit the *Enterprise*, penetrating the number 3 elevator, and exploded deep within the ship. Seconds later, a high-explosive bomb exploded on the deck aft and set fire to the 5-inch gun platform on the starboard side. Another high-explosive bomb struck amidships, blowing a 10-foot hole in the flight deck and putting the number 2 elevator out of action.

As the survivors of the first wave began to retire, the second wave of bombers attacked. Swarming fighters from the two carriers broke up their formation. A few redirected their attack to the *North Carolina*. Four bombs splashed close by, but none hit. Others dove on the *Enterprise*, scoring one near miss. By the time the Japanese strike force returned to their carriers, it was well after dark. Nineteen bombers and six Zeros failed to return.

Nagumo's second strike failed to locate Fletcher's carriers. The planes set a course based on sighting reports but ended up too far to the west. Fighter Direction Officers on board the *Enterprise* watched nervously as the planes passed by on their radar plots. When the aircraft returned to the Japanese carriers, it was after nightfall; four bombers were lost in the darkness. With the *Enterprise* seriously damaged, but able to make good speed, Fletcher withdrew to safety.

Kondō and Nagumo estimated that two U.S. carriers were seriously damaged and that Henderson Field would be unable to oppose Tanaka's landing. They ordered him to advance as Nagumo's carriers withdrew. Tanaka sent three destroyers ahead to bombard the airfield; they shelled Lunga Point by moonlight. The Marines sent dive bombers aloft to attack them, but neither side was very accurate.

At 0600, the Cactus Air Force took to the air. Within two hours it had sighted Tanaka's convoy and started its attack. His flagship, light cruiser *Jintsū*, was hit; Tanaka shifted his flag to the destroyer *Kagerō*. The *Kinryu Maru* was also hit, starting a fire that forced her abandonment. The *Boston Maru* suffered a damaging near miss. When the destroyer *Mutsuki* stopped to rescue survivors, a stick of bombs from a B-17 sank her. With his convoy irreparably crippled, Tanaka ordered a withdrawal. The first major Japanese effort to retake Guadalcanal had ended in defeat.

"BLOODY SEPTEMBER"

After the Battle of the Eastern Solomons, the campaign for Guadalcanal became one of attrition. Both sides struggled to resupply their garrisons on the island

---

Artillery on Edson's Ridge

Other Marines manning the scattered strongpoints around the division's perimeter watched the distant battle in awe. Seen from afar, the Ridge appeared to pulsate with yellow-orange explosions. Machine-gun tracer rounds split the night; ricochets spun away in bright tangents. Waves of gunfire and frenzied shouts would reach a dramatic crescendo, slowly fade, then build up again. The steady "boom" of the 11th Marines' howitzers echoed incessantly, each followed by its corresponding "*crump*" on impact. Pressure waves from the ceaseless explosions rocked the palms.

The Japanese had never faced artillery fire like this. Some of Kawaguchi's remnants would marvel at the Marines' "automatic artillery." Surviving officers of the Tamura Battalion (II/4) suspected the Marines had somehow positioned "sound detectors and automatic communication devices" along their approach path. Yet seismic intrusion devices lay two decades in the future. "Artillery Hell" for the Japanese the night of 13 September 1942 resulted not from high technology but from Merritt Edson's terrain analysis, [division artillery commander Colonel] Pedro del Valle's careful registration, the proficiency of the howitzer crews—and the dangerously fragile radio link between First Sergeant [Brice] Maddox at the point of attack to Corporal [Thomas] Watson at Edson's side, thence via phone line to the Raiders' switchboard and down the slope to the 11th Marines Fire Direction Center.

—COLONEL JOSEPH H. ALEXANDER, USMC (RET.), *EDSON'S RAIDERS: THE 1ST MARINE RAIDER BATTALION IN WORLD WAR II* (NAVAL INSTITUTE PRESS, 2010)

and gain the upper hand. The Tokyo Express brought more Japanese troops to the island by night, while Vice Admiral Ghormley supported the Marines with daylight missions covered by land-based aircraft and the Pacific Fleet's few operational carriers. On 31 August, that number was reduced by one when the *Saratoga* was torpedoed by submarine *I-26*. The carrier remained afloat but, like the *Enterprise*, was forced to leave the theater.

Lieutenant General Hyakutake, still focused on the campaign in New Guinea, continued to underestimate the strength of Vandegrift's forces. Hyakutake decided to commit Major General Kiyotake Kawaguchi's independent 35th Infantry Brigade, a seasoned force of 3,500 men. Kawaguchi and Tanaka disagreed on the best way to get the troops to Guadalcanal. Tanaka recommended high-speed nightly runs on board his destroyers; Kawaguchi preferred Army barges. They compromised and used both. Tanaka's destroyers would ferry Kawaguchi and the majority of his men; the 124th Infantry Regiment, under Colonel Akinosuke Oka would follow in the barges. The first echelon, about 750 men, were landed at Taivu Point on the night of 31 August. The following night, Kawaguchi joined them. Tanaka's Tokyo Express runs continued over the next several nights.

On 1 September, the Navy's 6th Naval Construction Battalion—Seabees—arrived on the island. It immediately started work on an auxiliary fighter strip to augment the existing runway, a task it would complete in a week's time. Two days later, Brigadier General Roy Geiger, commander of the 1st Marine Air Wing, arrived. Geiger took command of air operations at Cactus, with an eye toward maximizing its offensive potential.

One of his first accomplishments was locating and attacking Colonel Oka and his barges. In repeated bombing and strafing attacks, Oka lost more than half of his troops and the bulk of his supplies and equipment. Despite these losses, by the time Oka arrived on Guadalcanal, Kawaguchi had more than 6,000 men and was confident that his coordinated series of attacks would retake the airfield. He planned to sweep inland from his base at Taivu Point and attack Henderson Field from the south. Simultaneously, Oka's forces would attack from the west, Vandegrift, meanwhile,

A bomb explodes against the carrier *Enterprise*'s flight deck during the Battle of the Eastern Solomons, 24 August 1942. This was the third bomb to strike the ship in quick succession. The second started a fire in the 5-inch battery astern, visible in the upper left of this photograph. (National Archives)

underestimated the size of Kawaguchi's force. He suspected a fresh battalion would be enough to rout them, so on 8 September, he sent Colonel Edson with the 1st Raider Battalion and 1st Parachute Battalion to Taivu Point in a spoiling attack. They landed at the point and then pushed west, toward the village of Tasimboko. Kawaguchi, fearing a more substantial assault was coming, withdrew into the jungle. Edson's forces overwhelmed what little resistance they encountered, destroyed supplies and ammunition, and then withdrew. Vandegrift positioned them on the southern portion of his perimeter, along a ridge that Kawaguchi had identified as his objective.

To support Kawaguchi's advance, the Japanese air groups at Rabaul started raiding Guadalcanal daily on 9 September. Vice Admiral Kondō, with the *Shōkaku*, *Zuikaku*, and newly arrived light carrier *Zuihō*, sortied from Truk the same day, ready to pounce if the American carrier forces came out. These raids taxed the defenses of Henderson Field, but on 11 September additional planes and pilots arrived. Twenty-four Wildcats of VF-5, formerly part of the *Saratoga's* air wing, landed and began to operate from the new airstrip recently completed by the Seabees, "Fighter 1." Rear Admirals Turner and McCain also came to Cactus, to confer with Vandegrift and discuss plans for bringing the 7th Marines to Guadalcanal. The admirals and the fighters were in place just in time for the decisive push. Kawaguchi planned his main attack for the night of 12 September.

That evening a Japanese plane dropped a flare over Lunga Point, providing a point of aim for the light cruiser *Sendai* and the destroyers *Shikinami*, *Fubuki*, and *Suzukaze*. They bombarded Marine positions in coordination with Kawaguchi's assault from the south. His men came swarming out of the jungle, determined to seize commanding positions along what the Marines ultimately named "Edson's Ridge." The first night's battle was desperate and chaotic. Kawaguchi probed the Marine perimeter for weaknesses; Edson's men tried to channel his advance into fields of fire. By sunrise, both sides maintained their positions.

Rear Admiral Turner had seen enough. He officially recommended that the 7th Marines be transported to Guadalcanal immediately to augment Vandegrift's beleaguered garrison. He wanted the convoy to leave Espiritu Santo as soon as possible. On the morning of the 13th, Turner and McCain left to begin their preparations. That day, 18 additional Wildcats from the carriers *Wasp* and *Hornet* (CV-8) arrived. Cactus was becoming an "unsinkable aircraft carrier."

Kawaguchi's men started infiltrating into Marine positions as soon as it was dark, but the main assault began that night when a red signal rocket arced up from the trees and the Japanese came storming out of the jungle. Kawaguchi's advance broke through the defenders to the west of the ridge. Edson's men filled the breach, relying heavily on supporting artillery to break up Japanese concentrations. The fighting continued throughout the night, as the Japanese made determined thrusts against the Raiders and Paratroopers defending the ridge. At dawn, the last charge failed, and Kawaguchi's remaining men retreated. Roughly half his force was lost in the assault and the ensuing withdrawal back to Kokumbona. Edson's victory was "one of the crucial ground actions of the Pacific War," in the estimation of naval historian Samuel Eliot Morison. If Kawaguchi had broken through, the Marines would have lost the airfields, and with them their hold on the island. For his leadership during the battle, Edson was promoted to command of the 5th Marines and awarded the Medal of Honor. The final words of his citation read: "By his astute leadership and gallant devotion to duty, he enabled his men, despite severe losses, to cling tenaciously to their position on the vital ridge, thereby retaining command not only of the Guadalcanal airfield, but also of the 1st Division's entire offensive installations in the surrounding area."

On the 14th, Turner and the 7th Marines sailed from Espiritu Santo. To protect the reinforcement effort, Ghormley committed both of his carriers, the *Hornet* and *Wasp*. Apprehensive about enemy aerial attack and surface raids, Turner set a creative course to Guadalcanal. This delayed his arrival, exposing the carriers to greater risk. Commander Takaichi Kinashi's submarine *I-19* found the *Wasp* on the afternoon of 15 September and fired a salvo of six torpedoes. At least two hit the carrier, opening large holes in the hull and starting fires in the aviation gasoline tanks that triggered secondary explosions. The rapidly spreading conflagration doomed the *Wasp*. Another torpedo struck the destroyer *O'Brien* (DD-415), shattering her bow. The *North Carolina* was also hit, but she maintained station at 25 knots. For the remainder of September and most of October, the *Hornet* was the only U.S. carrier available in the Pacific.

The next day, Turner proceeded to Guadalcanal. A haze covered his advance and obscured his ships from Japanese patrols. By the morning of the 18th, Turner was unloading nearly 4,000 men of the 7th Marines along with their supporting arms and supplies. Before leaving, two of his destroyers shelled Japanese positions ashore.

THE BATTLE OF CAPE ESPERANCE

ON 28 SEPTEMBER, ADMIRAL NIMITZ ARRIVED IN NOUMÉA to confer with Vice Admiral Ghormley. The South Pacific area commander was fatigued; he seemed to lack the aggressive spirit required. Nimitz left the session concerned. The next day he flew on to Espiritu Santo and met with Rear Admiral Aubrey "Jake" Fitch, who was now air group commander in the South Pacific. From there Nimitz boarded a B-17 and flew to Guadalcanal, where he met with Vandegrift. Impressed with the fortitude of the Marine general's command, Nimitz promised to help. He prodded Ghormley to dispatch the 6,000 men of the Army's Americal (23rd Infantry) Division's 164th Infantry Regiment to the island.

Shattered wreckage of this ship, lying in the water off peaceful Cape Esperance, Guadalcanal, symbolizes the disaster that marked the turn of the Japanese tide of empire. (U.S. Naval Institute Photo Archive)

After the failure of Kawaguchi's effort, Lieutenant General Hyakutake was forced to admit that the Marine defenders on Guadalcanal were more capable than he had anticipated. The Imperial Army marshalled Lieutenant General Masao Maruyama's 2nd (Sendai) Division, which had fought in the Dutch East Indies, and committed it to Guadalcanal. Together with the IJN, the Japanese Army agreed to a determined effort to retake the island. In late September and early October, destroyers and barges brought Maruyama's division to Guadalcanal. It concentrated west of the Marine perimeter, where the majority of Kawaguchi's surviving men had coalesced. Colonel Edson's 5th Marine Regiment made spoiling attacks along the Matanikau River, but they failed to disrupt the Japanese timetable. On 9 October, Hyakutake transferred the 17th Army's headquarters to Guadalcanal so he could personally direct the offensive effort. He expected additional troops and supplies to arrive the night of 11 October.

At the same time, the 164th Infantry Regiment was being convoyed to the island by Rear Admiral Turner. The move would be covered by three separate task forces. The carrier *Hornet* provided distant cover from a position south of Guadalcanal. The battleship *Washington* (BB-56) and supporting forces hovered east of Malaita under Rear Admiral Willis A. Lee. TF 64, a cruiser-destroyer group under Rear Admiral Norman Scott, was ordered to protect the convoy by countering any Japanese moves into Ironbottom Sound.

Scott had four large cruisers and five destroyers. As they neared Guadalcanal, he received warning of an approaching Japanese force, led by Rear Admiral Aritomo Gotō. Gotō planned to bombard the airfield with his three heavy cruisers, the *Aoba*,

Norman Scott, pictured here as a captain while he was commanding officer of the cruiser *Pensacola* before the war. As a rear admiral, he led Task Force 64 into battle at Cape Esperance, surprising and overwhelming a Japanese bombardment force. (National Archives)

Furutaka, and *Kinugasa*. They were screened by two destroyers, the *Fubuki* and *Hatsuyuki*. Scott prepared to engage. He had spent the preceding weeks consistently practicing and drilling for night action. His ships and their crews had developed routines to combat the negative effects of fatigue and keep them alert through long hours. As TF 64 advanced toward Guadalcanal, it was well prepared.

SCOTT'S PLAN

Scott went into battle with a clear plan. Distributed formations had been problematic at night, both at the Battle of Savo Island and in prewar exercises, so he adopted an extremely concentrated formation. Scott placed his ships in a single line, with three destroyers in the front, his cruisers in the center, and two destroyers in the rear. This was a shift away from prewar tactics, which emphasized looser formations that allowed destroyers to close for torpedo attacks while cruisers supported them from longer range with gunfire. Scott chose the line for three major reasons: to ease coordination, reduce the risk of friendly fire, and maximize his firepower. He considered it "most practical for night action."

Scott called his formation a "double header" because he expected to be able to fight on both flanks—the van and rear—simultaneously. He wanted to avoid being surprised, so he ordered the rear cruisers and destroyers to open fire on the disengaged flank without orders. The simplicity of a single column allowed each ship to keep station by conforming to the movements of the ship in front, making it much easier to coordinate movements at night. If he could maneuver his line effectively, Scott would be able to bring a heavy fire on the enemy.

As Scott's formation entered Savo Sound, the destroyers *Farenholt* (DD-491), *Duncan* (DD-485), and *Laffey* (DD-459) were in the van, followed by Scott's flagship the *San Francisco* (CA-38) and the cruisers *Boise* (CL-47), *Salt Lake City* (CA-25), and *Helena* (CL-50). The destroyers *Buchanan* (DD-484) and *McCalla* (DD-488) followed. Scott's destroyer commander was Captain Robert G. Tobin, leader of Destroyer Squadron (DesRon) 12. He flew his flag in the lead destroyer *Farenholt*. Captain Gilbert C. Hoover noted the conditions from the bridge of *Helena*:

The weather conditions were average to good. Wind was light blowing from 128 degrees true, velocity fourteen knots. Sea was smooth of about force two with swells from 225 degrees. The moon was in its first quarter, setting early in the night. The sky was clear except to northwest from which direction a great deal of "heat lightning" was noted all night. Due to having a land background upon passing between Guadalcanal and Russell Islands, visibility was poor both due to darkness and lack of sea horizon.

—CAPTAIN GILBERT C. HOOVER, USS *HELENA*, 20 OCTOBER 1942

Scott's Orders to TF 64

Cruisers form dog [column] to facilitate signals, destroyers divided three ahead [and] remainder astern rear cruiser. Destroyers illuminate as soon after radar contact as possible, fire torpedoes at large ships and gun destroyers and small craft. Cruisers maintain continuous fire at short ranges on small ship targets instead of full gun salvoes with large intervals. Number 3 and 4 cruisers and rear destroyers keep watch on disengaged flank [and] open fire without order. Destroyers in van keep alert to cruiser change of course in event TBS [radio] fails. Changes of course may be numerous. Be alert for turn signals by TBS or blinker. Keep TBS adequately manned and circuit [as] clear as possible.

—REAR ADMIRAL NORMAN SCOTT, COMMANDER TASK FORCE 64, "MEMORANDUM FOR TASK GROUP 64.2"

Captain E. J. Moran of the cruiser *Boise* recorded similar observations; horizontal visibility was limited to about 5,000 yards.

The *Helena* and *Boise* were the two most modern cruisers in Scott's formation. They were near-sister ships; the *Boise* was a member of the *Brooklyn* class and the *Helena* was a slightly improved version with a more powerful secondary battery. Both were equipped with the Navy's most effective surface search radar, the SG, which gave them a much better sense of their surroundings. Their main batteries had 15 6-inch guns, and they could fire them continuously, with each gun firing as soon as it was ready. FC radars would ensure each gun fired accurately.

Scott chose the older heavy cruiser *San Francisco* as his flagship. His choice made sense; the *San Francisco* had been built to operate as a flagship and had the necessary facilities for the admiral, his staff, and a dedicated flag plot. The *Helena* and *Boise* did not. The flag plot was expected to track the developing situation—the movements of Scott's ships and enemy

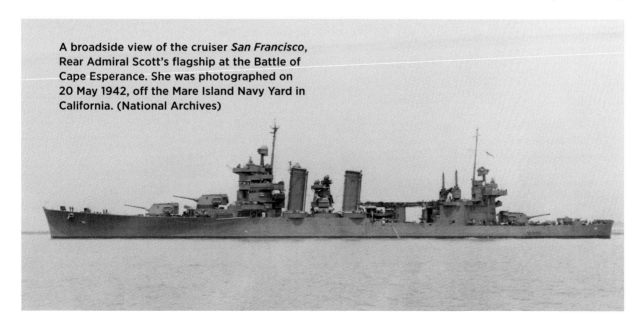

A broadside view of the cruiser *San Francisco*, Rear Admiral Scott's flagship at the Battle of Cape Esperance. She was photographed on 20 May 1942, off the Mare Island Navy Yard in California. (National Archives)

The destroyer *Farenholt*, Captain Robert G. Tobin's flagship as commander of Destroyer Squadron 12 at the Battle of Cape Esperance. She is pictured on 24 August 1942 while receiving supplies from the carrier *Wasp*. Note her Measure 12 (modified) camouflage scheme. (National Archives)

contacts—so the admiral could give clear orders. However, technology had outpaced the processes involved. The *San Francisco* had only an SC radar, not an SG, and Scott turned it off because he feared the Japanese would be able to detect its signals. He relied on the *San Francisco*'s FC radars and reports from his other ships—such as the *Helena* and *Boise*—to give him a view of the world around him. This is one reason he placed so much emphasis on keeping the radio frequency clear; it was essential for his situational awareness.

Scott's force faced another problem. As detailed as his drills and plans were, his ships still went into combat with a degree of uncertainty. There was no clear sense of when and how the destroyers would attack with torpedoes. Should they act on their own initiative when targets appeared, or should they hold back and wait for orders?

There was also uncertainty about when and how to open fire. The rear ships could open fire on the disengaged flank without orders, but what about other circumstances? Would Scott give the order, or would individual ships open fire when the enemy was in range? Soon, Scott and his captains would face these questions directly.

"ROGER!"

Scott patrolled outside Ironbottom Sound, west of Cape Esperance and Savo Island, correctly anticipating that the Japanese would head between them. As the ships of Goto's bombardment group approached, the SG radar on the *Helena* located them. First contact was made at 2325 at a range of 27,700 yards; her crew tracked the target for 15 minutes before reporting to the admiral. In the meantime, Scott remained unaware of the developing situation.

The *Boise* running trials in 1938. She was a *Brooklyn*-class light cruiser, armed with 15 6-inch guns in five triple turrets. These guns could fire extremely rapidly, making the *Boise* and her sisters very formidable in close-range actions. (Naval History and Heritage Command)

34

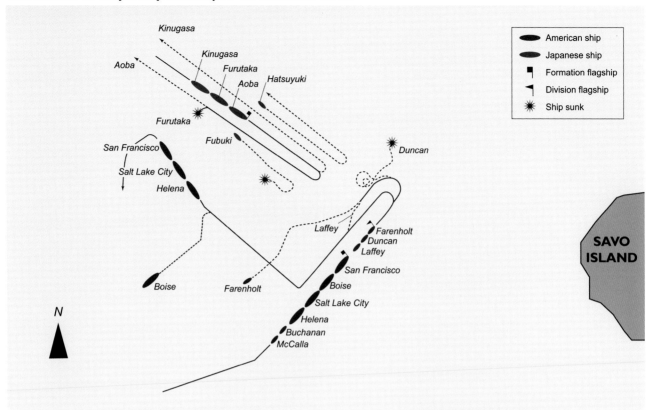

⬛	American ship
⬬	Japanese ship
⬛⚑	Formation flagship
⬛⚐	Division flagship
✳	Ship sunk

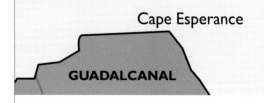

SAVO ISLAND

Cape Esperance

GUADALCANAL

Order of Battle: Cape Esperance

Navy Forces - Rear Admiral Norman Scott

Van Destroyers
  Farenholt (Captain Robert G. Tobin)
  Duncan
  Laffey

Cruisers
  San Francisco (flag)
  Boise
  Salt Lake City
  Helena

Rear Destroyers
  Buchanan
  McCalla

IJN Forces - Rear Admiral Aritomo Gotō

Bombardment Cruiser Unit
  Aoba (flag)
  Furutaka
  Kinugasa

Destroyer Screen
  Fubuki
  Hatsuyuki

Ensign Gash, the radar officer [on board the *Helena*], looked over the operator's shoulder. Together they watched the scope. The twinkle began to appear with every sweep of the spoke; then it began to persist after the spoke had passed and developed finally into a small, glowing dot which remained in view. Gash notified the open bridge.
—CAPTAIN CHARLES COOK, USN (RET.), *THE BATTLE OF CAPE ESPERANCE: ENCOUNTER AT GUADALCANAL* (NAVAL INSTITUTE PRESS, 1992)

While Gash observed Gotō's approaching formation, Scott, at 2332, ordered a reversal of course. His ships were approaching the northern limits of their patrol line and he wanted to keep them athwart the entrance to Savo Sound. The order was executed at 2333 and the American line turned through 180 degrees to come about on a southwesterly course. Scott's line turned in two

The light cruiser *Helena* off Mare Island Navy Yard on 1 July 1942. She has been repaired and refitted after the Pearl Harbor raid and is on her way to the South Pacific. Note that wartime censors have obliterated her radars. The *Helena*'s SG radar operators were consistently the most effective search team in the Battle of Cape Esperance and First Naval Battle of Guadalcanal on 12–13 November. (Naval History and Heritage Command)

The cruiser *Kinugasa* as she appeared before her prewar modernization (October 1938–November 1940). Her outward appearance was similar during the war. Her captain, Masao Sawa, recognizing that Rear Admiral Scott's cruisers had seriously damaged the *Aoba* and *Furutaka* as they came about, changed course to port instead of following around in their wake. This decision likely saved his ship. The *Kinugasa* was lost and Sawa was killed on 14 November 1942. (U.S. Naval Institute Photo Archive)

pieces, often considered a mistake. The lead destroyer, the *Farenholt*, and Scott's flagship, *San Francisco*, began sweeping to port simultaneously, creating a break in the line. If it was a mistake, then it was an error on board the flagship because she did not wait and follow in the wake of the van destroyers. This is possible but unlikely. Navy formations often maneuvered as separate units, and it is probable that Scott, who believed his greatest offensive strength was the guns of his cruisers, wanted to keep them unmasked. Had the cruisers waited to turn and followed behind the destroyers, the cruisers would have been in the middle of the turn, and unable to bring their guns to bear, when the Japanese came into range.

Regardless, the timing of the turn was crucial. It kept Scott across Gotō's path, but it also led to significant confusion. As the cruisers came onto the new course, the rear destroyers followed in their wake. The van destroyers accelerated and traced a wide path to port, to bring them parallel to the cruiser column and on its starboard side. That was the configuration of Scott's formation when the contact reports started to stream in from various radars and lookouts.

Gotō's force was arranged in a "T." His three cruisers were in a line, with his flagship *Aoba* in the lead, followed by the *Furutaka* and *Kinugasa*. The two destroyers were arranged on the flanks, slightly ahead of the flagship. The *Hatsuyuki* was to port and the *Fubuki* to starboard. Since Scott had kept his force hidden from Japanese search planes, Gotō did not expect to encounter opposition. The only other ships he thought were in the sound were Rear Admiral Takaji Joshima's reinforcement group with the two seaplane carriers *Chitose* and *Nisshin* (burdened by more than 700 soldiers, heavy guns, supplies, and ammunition) escorted by six destroyers.

The *Helena*'s contact report made it to Scott at 2342. By this time, the *Helena*'s crew was confident they had located an enemy formation; the contact had resolved into at least three separate ships and fire control radars were on and tracking. Scott lacked these details. He was afraid the *Helena*'s radar had picked up Tobin's van destroyers, which were on a similar bearing. Uncertain as to the developing situation, Scott hesitated and attempted to locate the three van destroyers. He asked Tobin if he was regaining position at the head of the column. Tobin replied, "Affirmative; coming up on your starboard flank." Scott's poor situational awareness cost valuable time.

In the meantime, on board the *Salt Lake City*, gunnery officer Lieutenant Commander James T. Brewer received word of the approaching contacts. The first report came from a sharp-eyed lookout, Master-at-Arms McKinley Bland; Bland had exceptional night vision

and had been hand-picked. Additional reports came into Brewer as the range closed. Captain Ernest G. Small, the *Salt Lake City*'s commanding officer, entered the chart house, home to the SC radar display. Small asked Lieutenant (junior grade) Chester M. Lee, the radar officer, about the contact. Lee was confident it was an enemy ship; he had tracked the signal and knew it was not Tobin's destroyers.

Captain Edward J. Moran on board the *Boise* also recognized the danger. Her radars had detected Gotō's force at 2338, when it was 14,000 yards away. Moran received word a minute later. There were five different "pips" on the *Boise*'s SG display, and one of them was suspected to be two ships. Moran ordered his fire control radars to select targets; the FC locked onto the largest one, believed to be a cruiser at the head of the enemy formation. The FD focused on what appeared to be a destroyer. At 2344, Moran sent word to Scott that the *Boise* had five "bogies" on her radar screen. This term was confusing; Scott and his staff assumed "bogies" meant airplanes.

At the same time, the *San Francisco*'s aft FC radar, which had been ordered to locate the reported contacts,

The heavy cruiser *Salt Lake City* under way during the 1930s. She was the first of the U.S. Navy's interwar "treaty cruisers." Her design emphasized speed and firepower. (Naval History and Heritage Command)

found one of the Japanese ships. It was 5,000 yards away to the northwest. Very soon thereafter, visual contact was made with an unidentified destroyer. Captain Charles H. "Soc" McMorris recorded the uncertainty on board the flagship at this time.

> Inasmuch as positions of own destroyers were not known with certainty, there was some reluctance to open fire on ships whose hostile characters were not clearly known. *Farenholt*, *Duncan*, and *Laffey* were known to be proceeding up the starboard side of the cruiser column but it was not known how far they had progressed nor their distance from the cruiser column.
>
> —CAPTAIN CHARLES H. McMORRIS, USS *SAN FRANCISCO*, 31 OCTOBER 1942

The other ships in Scott's formation had a much better sense of the approaching danger. Although he had explicitly ordered ships on the disengaged flank to open fire immediately, his captains expected Scott to take the lead when the enemy was headed straight for them. Captain Hoover realized it would be dangerous to wait any longer. At 2346, he requested permission to open fire. "Roger" was the code word for opening fire, but it was also used to acknowledge receipt of a message. When the *Helena*'s "Interrogatory Roger" came over the TBS radio, the *San Francisco* responded with "Roger," intending to acknowledge receipt. The *Helena*'s crew understood it as permission to open fire. The cruiser lashed out with her main and secondary batteries.

> At 2346 commenced firing and fire was immediately opened to starboard in continuous fire. The range of the target at commence firing was 3600 yards, bearing about 100 [degrees] relative. Bearing continued to draw to the right and range decreased to 2850 yards at which time it began to open. Fire was continued for about two minutes at which time "check fire" was ordered. At about 2348 the target disappeared completely from the FC and SG radar screens. No ship was visible at the point of aim, however a dense cloud of smoke, with occasional glow of flame was visible at this point.
>
> —CAPTAIN GILBERT C. HOOVER, USS *HELENA*, 20 OCTOBER 1942

The other ships in column followed suit. Moments after Captain Small left the chart house, convinced of the hostile nature of the approaching contacts, the *Salt Lake City* opened fire. The fire moved up the American column from the rear; the *Boise* was next.

> Commenced firing with both batteries immediately following *Salt Lake City*. The main battery concentrated with *Salt Lake City* on the leading enemy ship, in continuous fire, using radar train and ranges, at a range of approximately 4500 yards, bearing 324 degrees true. Hits were observed in the first salvo, which was a short straddle. Fire was maintained with a spot of up 100, and in a relatively short time the target was lighted up by a fire amidships. She was tentatively identified by several officers as a *Nati* [sic] class heavy cruiser. Our gunfire was apparently very effective at this short range, and the target was hit almost continuously.
>
> —CAPTAIN EDWARD J. MORAN, USS *BOISE*, 22 OCTOBER 1942

Scott was shocked. He was unaware that Captain Hoover had asked permission to open fire. The TBS operators on board his flagship had not realized that their acknowledgement had been interpreted as an order to do so. As the gunfire moved up the column, the *San Francisco*'s gunners, confident of their targets, opened fire as well.

> At about 2347 commenced firing with main and secondary batteries on an unidentified enemy ship bearing 300 degrees true (90 degrees relative), range 4600 yards. In accordance with doctrine, this was the left hand ship that had been located. After several salvoes the target ship and another ship close to it were observed to be on fire, one burning severely. Fire was shifted to a destroyer thought to be of the *Amagiri* class, which was approaching the ship from the starboard beam. This destroyer suffered one or more hits from our 5-in and a glow from the damage continued between his stacks.
>
> —CAPTAIN CHARLES H. McMORRIS, USS *SAN FRANCISCO*, 31 OCTOBER 1942

Scott was right to be concerned about Tobin's van destroyers. Although he had not sighted the Japanese, Tobin recognized that he was in a dangerous position. He thought the best course of action would be to turn and join the line astern of the cruisers. Then the *Helena* opened fire.

> Before any action could be taken toward turning to take position astern of cruisers, fire was opened by own forces, shells at first going over the top of this vessel, the fire being about abeam of the cruisers. Consideration was then given toward the best way to get out of this unfavorable position and decision was made to continue at best speed and pull out ahead

The *Buchanan* refuels from the carrier *Wasp* while on the way to the invasion of Guadalcanal, 3 August 1942. The *Buchanan* was one of Scott's rear destroyers at the Battle of Cape Esperance. She wears the Measure 12 (modified) camouflage scheme. (National Archives)

as a turn to the left would throw us into our own cruisers and to the right into the enemy.

—CAPTAIN ROBERT G. TOBIN, COMDESRON 12, USS *FARENHOLT*, 23 OCTOBER 1942

If Tobin was surprised, Rear Admiral Gotō was alarmed and angry. He was convinced that his ships had accidentally run into Rear Admiral Joshima's reinforcement group and that the firing was due to mistaken identification. He ordered a column movement to the right, to move away from the gunfire and open his broadsides, but he remained unaware that he was a victim of U.S. gunnery. Gotō died cursing sour luck and incompetence as shells slammed into the *Aoba*'s bridge.

Scott was also confused. Unaware of the confidence of his captains, and still uncertain as to the presence of the enemy, Scott feared his cruisers were firing at Tobin's destroyers. He ordered a cease-fire.

At 2347 order for all ships to cease firing was heard over voice radio. CTG 64.2 [Admiral Scott] inquired

if I was all right, reply being made in the affirmative. About 30 seconds later reported that our own units were firing on us. Fire of own units decreased in volume but continued.

—CAPTAIN ROBERT G. TOBIN, COMDESRON 12, USS *FARENHOLT*, 23 OCTOBER 1942

Many of Scott's ships, sure of their targets, kept firing. Although Captain Moran of the *Boise* indicated he checked fire around this time, he did it to ensure his guns were still on and tracking, not because he doubted the identity of his targets. Captain Hoover also checked fire, but for similar reasons. On board the *San Francisco*, the situation was more confused. Her primary target at the time was an enemy destroyer, the *Fubuki*, which resembled a U.S. ship in the darkness.

Cease firing was ordered by Comtaskgroup 64.2 [Admiral Scott] who felt it was our own destroyer (the general appearance and camouflage was similar to our two-stackers). This order was delivered personally

Rear Admiral Aritomo Gotō's damaged flagship, the heavy cruiser *Aoba*, anchored off Buin in the Shortlands on 13 October 1942. Gotō was killed on her bridge during the Battle of Cape Esperance. The *Aoba* would leave for Truk later that evening and ultimately arrive at Kure for extensive repairs on 22 October. (U.S. Naval Institute Photo Archive)

by word of mouth as well as by the TBS. Firing was ceased and destroyer closed into about 1400 yards and paralleled this ship to starboard. Destroyer flashed a blinker gun or floodlight on the water in direction of this ship and made some undistinguishable character. One white over one red lights were turned on.

—CAPTAIN CHARLES H. McMORRIS, USS *SAN FRANCISCO*, 31 OCTOBER 1942

The lights were recognition signals. The crew of the *Fubuki*, like Rear Admiral Gotō, assumed the reinforcement group was firing upon them. Scott's men had the advantage; the brief pause allowed them to be more certain of their targets. They quickly resumed fire.

After . . . destroyer turned away and was then illuminated by searchlight, and two white bands around forward stack could be clearly seen, along with a lattice type foremast and other definitely Japanese characteristics. Fire was resumed with main and secondary batteries, but only after destroyer had succeeded in turning about 90 degrees to starboard opening the range to 2600 yards and gone to high speed (estimated 25 to 30 knots). . . . The target angle at commence firing

was 180 degrees. The second 8-in salvo straddled. The destroyer stopped, burned violently for a few moments, exploded, turned on its side and sank.

—CAPTAIN CHARLES H. McMORRIS, USS *SAN FRANCISCO*, 31 OCTOBER 1942

The *Fubuki*, hit by several ships, exploded and sank at about 2353. Gotō's other ships were in a similarly desperate situation. Scott's turn to keep his cruisers athwart

Damage to the *Aoba* and the Sinking of the *Furutaka*

The *Aoba* was hit by some twenty-four 6-in and 8-in shells between 2346 and about 0010, just before and while turning with the *Furutaka* to starboard. Eight officers were killed, including Rear Admiral Gotō Aritomo ... and two staff officers, along with seventy-one enlisted men. Hits were scored on the compass bridge (mortally wounding Gotō); the Type 94 main gun director; Number 2 turret (out of use); Number 3 turret (destroyed by an explosion and burned out); the port Type 94 HA [High-Angle] director; Number 2 (port forward) 12-cm HA-gun mount; Number 2 (port) searchlight tower; the catapult; Number 2 boiler room, putting four boilers out of commission; the foremast, which fell on and damaged Number 1 (starboard forward) 12-cm HA-gun mount; and nonvital areas along the port side of the hull above the waterline and the port superstructure.

the entrance to Savo Sound had allowed him to cross the Japanese "T." While all the broadsides of the American cruisers could bear, only the forward turrets of the Japanese cruisers could come into action and, except for the *Aoba*, their forward arcs were obscured by the ship ahead. Gotō's final order to turn to starboard helped address this situation, but as his first two cruisers came around, each moved through the same position in the water, allowing Scott's cruisers to concentrate on them in succession. The *Aoba* was crippled. Hits knocked out two of her three turrets, shattered her bridge, and destroyed one of her boiler rooms.

The next cruiser in column, the *Furutaka*, was hit even more severely. Shells pounded into her turrets and torpedo battery. Fires within the torpedo battery were fed by the oxygen supply for the Type 93s and burned out of control. Flames provided a clear point of aim for American gunners. The cumulative damage proved fatal.

Captain Masao Sawa of the *Kinugasa*, recognizing that the U.S. ships had wrecked the preceding cruisers as they swept through the starboard turn, changed course to port, away from Scott's line. This kept his ship obscured in the darkness beyond the burning *Aoba* and *Furutaka*, where she remained relatively unscathed.

Captain Tobin brought his destroyers into the fight. The *Farenholt* opened fire at 2349 on an enemy vessel "brilliantly illuminated by starshells" and her captain, Lieutenant Commander Eugene T. Seaward, gave orders to launch torpedoes at favorable targets. On board the *Laffey*, Lieutenant Commander William E. Hank sought to extricate his ship from its vulnerable position. He ordered full emergency astern and turned hard to port, attempting to fall into Scott's line behind the *Helena*. While these maneuvers were under way, Hank opened fire on the *Aoba* with three of his 5-inch guns; the fourth illuminated the Japanese column with starshells.

Lieutenant Commander Edmund B. Taylor, the *Duncan*'s skipper, had other ideas. Alone among the van destroyers, he had sighted the approaching Japanese during the reversal of course. Rather than following the *Laffey* through the course change, Taylor increased speed and headed toward Gotō's column to make a close-range torpedo attack. He picked the *Furutaka*

The destroyer *Usugumo* was a sister ship of the *Fubuki*. The *Fubuki* was destroyed by gunfire from Rear Admiral Scott's force. (U.S. Naval Institute Photo Archive)

The *Furutaka* was hit by several 6-in and 8-in shells between 2349 and 0005 on 11 October. At 2349 a hit wrecked Number 3 20-cm turret, and at 2351 Number 2 (port) torpedo-tube mount was hit. The Type 93 oxygen-propelled torpedoes in the tubes ignited and started heavy fires, which attracted the gunfire of the U.S. ships. At 2354 the forward starboard and at 2355 the aft port engine rooms were hit, and the ship slowed. At 0005 the forward port engine room was hit, and the main steam line to the remaining engine room was pierced. All power was lost, and the *Furutaka* flooded slowly despite the crew's efforts to keep her afloat and get her moving. After a two-hour struggle the order was given at 0208 on 12 October to abandon ship. The evacuation was completed at 0220, and the *Furutaka* sank stern first at 0228, bearing 310 degrees at 22 miles from Savo Island.

—ADAPTED FROM ERIC LACROIX AND LINTON WELLS II, *JAPANESE CRUISERS OF THE PACIFIC WAR* (NAVAL INSTITUTE PRESS, 1997)

The heavy cruiser *Furutaka* on 9 June 1939, running high speed trials after her reconstruction. The *Furutaka* succumbed to the combined fire of U.S. cruisers and destroyers during the Battle of Cape Esperance. (U.S. Naval Institute Photo Archive)

out of the enemy line and swung to starboard to open his torpedo arcs. When the *Furutaka* also turned right, following the flagship around, she opened the range. Taylor turned back to the left to pursue. A shell hit in a boiler room reduced her speed; it was the first of many. The *Duncan* was between the two task forces, and enemy ships were on both bows. Taylor's ship was caught in a crossfire. Additional hits destroyed the gun director, knocked over the forward stack, and started a fire in one of the forward ammunition handling rooms. Lieutenant (junior grade) Robert L. Fowler, the torpedo officer, managed to fire one torpedo at the *Furutaka* before he was mortally wounded; his men got off a second, but then their mount was wrecked. Both torpedoes missed. Taylor, aware that he was being hit by ships from both sides, turned on his recognition lights just before another salvo slammed into the destroyer. It knocked out all electrical power. The *Duncan*, mortally wounded and with fires raging on her forecastle, steamed circles in the darkness.

The *Farenholt* was also subjected to a dangerous crossfire.

At 2350 the *Farenholt* was hit on the fore yard arm and at the top of Number Two stack. Fragments from latter hit jammed the torpedo mount amidships. At the same time or shortly thereafter, the *Farenholt* was struck at water line on port side near Frame 65 by one or more shells. This hit put the I.C. [interior communications] and Plotting Room, [sic] out of commission. This hit and one at water line, port side, Frame 85, disrupted all power, lighting, and communications in forward part of ship. At this time the *Farenholt* was about abreast of *San Francisco*. Area was cleared, crossing ahead of *San Francisco*, which cruiser was apparently turning to starboard to close the enemy.

—CAPTAIN ROBERT G. TOBIN, COMDESRON 12, USS *FARENHOLT*, 23 OCTOBER 1942

The hits on the port side were from U.S. guns. They were "apparently 6-in" and so were likely fired by the *Boise* or *Helena*. The two destroyers at the rear of the column also joined in the battle. Lieutenant Commander William G. Cooper of the *McCalla* trained her guns on the burning enemy cruisers while Commander

The destroyer *Duncan* on the way from her builder's yard at Kearny, New Jersey, on 15 April 1942. Note her camouflage scheme. The *Duncan* was caught in a crossfire and sunk at the Battle of Cape Esperance. (Naval History and Heritage Command)

Ralph E. Wilson of the *Buchanan* "shot the works." She fired five torpedoes at the enemy, along with a steady stream of 5-inch shells. At about 2354, one of the torpedoes slammed into the *Furutaka*, adding to her misery.

At the same time, Scott turned his column to starboard, to come west and parallel the track of the *Aoba* and *Furutaka* as they attempted to withdraw. The *Boise* engaged with one of these ships, likely the crippled *Furutaka*.

> Reports from several stations suggest that she may have been firing some overs, as the whistling of projectiles overhead was observed. Later, she straddled, and splashes were observed 50 feet short, as well as to port. Shorts threw considerable water over starboard A.A. [antiaircraft] battery and after superstructure.
>
> —CAPTAIN EDWARD J. MORAN, USS *BOISE*, 22 OCTOBER 1942

Three or four hits followed. One 8-inch shell struck the *Boise*'s side armor and exploded without penetrating, but the blast dented the armor and opened holes above the armor plating. A group of smaller shells hit the superstructure. One exploded on impact, spraying Number 3 5-inch gun with shrapnel and causing several casualties. The others burst inside the captain's cabin, demolishing it and starting a fire. But the enemy ship seemed to get the worst of it. Moran reported that the "target burst into flames and burned very brightly" and that it was "enveloped in smoke."

The *Boise* ceased firing at about 2357. Scott ordered another cease-fire right around midnight to try to make sense of the situation and assess the progress of the battle: "At midnight it appeared to me that some shaking down was necessary in order to continue our attack successfully. We flashed battle lights and allowed ten minutes to rectify the formation, and then changed course to 290 degrees true, toward the enemy." On board the *Helena*, radar operators were tracking the lone undamaged Japanese cruiser, the *Kinugasa*.

> At about this time radar plot, the plotting room and Director 1 reported that there was an enemy ship bearing about 095 degrees relative, range about 9000 yards, tracking gave a course of 320 degrees true and speed of 30 knots, that it was trying to get away.
>
> —CAPTAIN GILBERT C. HOOVER, USS *HELENA*, 20 OCTOBER 1942

Captain Sawa was trying to get away, but he was prepared to fight his way out. From his concealed position,

he had fired torpedoes toward the American column. They appeared ahead of the *Boise* a few minutes after Scott's cease-fire order.

> A torpedo wake ahead was reported. Ship was brought to the right with hard rudder to parallel its track, and apparently the port bow just cleared the torpedo. A second torpedo was observed passing aft along the starboard side, and the stern swung clear of it [by] about 30 yards. Dissemination of the report of "torpedo approaching" was general throughout the ship; the news of its missing was received with great relief, especially from below-decks stations.
>
> —CAPTAIN EDWARD J. MORAN, USS *BOISE*, 22 OCTOBER 1942

The *Boise* avoided significant damage from the torpedoes, but the lull in the firing had allowed Sawa's men to identify targets in the U.S. line and develop a good fire control solution; at 0009 the *Kinugasa* opened fire with her 8-inch guns.

> We were engaged by a heavy cruiser firing from forward of the beam (about 045 degrees relative) well separated from presumed enemy position. It is

The *Suichūdan* Hits the *Boise*

An 8-in shell . . . penetrated hull at frame 31, starboard, 9 feet below the waterline, and exploded in the large 6-in magazine between turret Number 1 and Number 2 handling rooms. The blast of this explosion penetrated all forward main battery magazines and handling rooms except turret Number 3 handling room, which, however, was rendered untenable by flames entering through forward scuttle propelled by blast. Burning gases were propelled up through turrets Number 1 and Number 2 setting them both afire. All magazine and handling room personnel except those in turret Number 3 handling room were killed, as were all men in turret Number 2 and survivors inside turret Number 1. The effect of this hit on the weather decks was spectacular, flaming gases torching from apertures in turrets Number 1 and 2, setting the forecastle deck afire, burning personnel who had just escaped turret Number 1 gun room, and illuminating the entire area. Adjacent ships considered the *Boise* lost.

—CAPTAIN E. J. MORAN, USS *BOISE*, 22 OCTOBER 1942

believed that this ship was not a part of the original enemy formation. Between 0009 and 0012 she fired at *Boise* unopposed, shooting beautifully with twin 8-in mounts. She straddled us repeatedly along the forward half of the forecastle, and made two known hits, the first in the barbette of turret Number 1 at 0010 and the second through the side below the armor, into the 6-in magazine between turrets Number 1 and Number 2 handling rooms at 0011.

—CAPTAIN E. J. MORAN, USS *BOISE*, 22 OCTOBER 1942

The first hit exploded inside the gun room of Turret Number 1, and the turret officer gave the order to abandon it. Eleven men escaped; the remaining forty-four were killed. The second hit was more devastating. The *Kinugasa* hit the *Boise* with a *suichūdan*, a diving shell that struck the water and then traveled underwater, penetrating the hull of the ship below the waterline. This shell exploded in the 6-inch magazine and started a terrific conflagration.

Scott thought the *Boise* was in trouble: "The fire on her forecastle was so intense and of such size at one instant that I feared we might lose her." Moran recognized the danger to his ship and ordered the forward magazine flooded, but the men who would have carried out the order had been killed. The flames grew and threatened to detonate the magazine. The ship was saved by water rushing in through the hole opened by the *suichūdan*; the water extinguished the fire in the magazine before a detonation could occur. The *Boise*, crippled, sheered out of line.

Captain Small maneuvered the *Salt Lake City* to interpose her between the Japanese and Moran's burning cruiser. The *Salt Lake City* and *Kinugasa* engaged in a duel for the next several minutes. Two shells hit the American cruiser; one glanced off the armor while another detonated in a fireroom, killing one man and doing minor damage. The *Kinugasa* was also lightly struck. While the *Salt Lake City* tried to exact revenge on the *Boise*'s assailant, the *Helena* continued to pour her fire into Gotō's flagship, *Aoba*.

Our target was observed to be on fire aft and to have several explosions. Shortly afterward it seemed to burst wide open with one terrific explosion and then disappeared. Fire was ceased at about 0012 by both batteries. The target disappeared from sight and from all radar screens. At least two observers (director range-

The *Boise*, listing and damaged from the Battle of Cape Esperance, arrives at Philadelphia Navy Yard for repairs in November 1942. (National Archives)

UNITED STATES NAVAL INSTITUTE

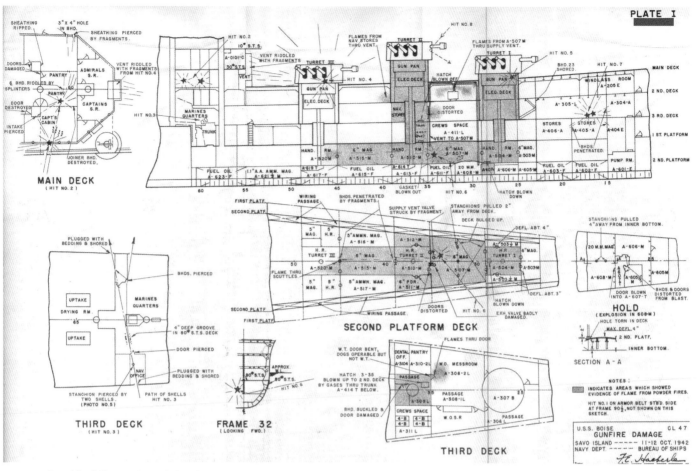

PLATE I

Graphical illustration of the damage to *Boise* at the Battle of Cape Esperance. (From *War Damage Report No. 24*)

finder operator and director pointer) state that this last target was a cruiser with three or four forward turrets.

—CAPTAIN GILBERT C. HOOVER, USS *HELENA*, 20 OCTOBER 1942

These reports were optimistic, but the *Aoba* survived to withdraw. The *San Francisco* momentarily fired on the retiring *Kinugasa*: "Another ship was briefly sighted through the smoke and the glare. This ship was believed to be a three-stack cruiser. It was picked up by radar and although never again sighted was taken under fire using radar control exclusively. Radar showed several straddled in range, but no observation could be made in deflection and no hits or explosions were observed."

By 0025, the battle was over. Scott and his cruisers ceased fire. The *Fubuki* was gone; the *Hatsuyuki* was standing by the crippled *Furutaka*, ready to take off survivors; and Gotō's two remaining cruisers were withdrawing. At 0028, Scott changed course to southsouthwest and began to regroup. Most of the cruisers formed up, but initially, there was no response from the *Boise*, *Farenholt*, or *Duncan*. Lieutenant Commander Cooper's *McCalla* was dispatched to look after them.

Captain Moran's *Boise* joined Scott's formation as it retired out of the sound; her crew had done an impressive job extinguishing the fires, and she was able to make 20 knots. Ultimately, the *Boise* went to Philadelphia for repairs, where she received a celebratory welcome. The *Farenholt* also retired from Ironbottom Sound, but more slowly, escorted by the destroyer *Aaron Ward* (DD-483). The *McCalla* looked after the *Duncan*; for a time, it seemed she might be saved, but progressive flooding convinced all hands it was hopeless. She went down shortly before noon.

RESULTS OF SCOTT'S VICTORY

Scott had broken the image of the Japanese as unassailable masters of night combat. In a situation with remarkable parallels to Savo Island two months earlier, nearly complete surprise had delivered victory. Like Vice Admiral Mikawa, Scott had maintained the cohesion of his force through complicated maneuvers and achieved his primary objective: defeat of enemy surface forces. But also like Mikawa, Scott had failed to interfere with enemy landing operations. While Gotō's

The destroyer *McCalla* being delivered to the Navy by Federal Shipbuilding and Dry Dock Company on 26 May 1942. She was the last ship in Scott's formation at Cape Esperance. After the battle, the *McCalla* stood by the *Duncan*, rescuing survivors while the damaged destroyer went down. (National Archives)

force was being decimated off Cape Esperance, Rear Admiral Joshima was successfully landing his troops and supplies at Tassafaronga. Those men, and the artillery that came with them, would make the situation more difficult for Vandegrift's defenders.

On the tactical level, Scott's victory suggested that the linear formation was a valid solution to the difficulty of coordinating task forces at night. Scott reported: "The column formation proved to be very satisfactory to carry out our task. All ships fired at targets of opportunity and there was practically no cross firing or interference. In a very short time four enemy ships were seen badly on fire." But these initial appearances were deceptive. Scott was fortunate to position his line across the path of the approaching Japanese so that he could bring the firepower of his whole formation to bear. He also benefitted from the element of surprise. In the next major action, Scott's linear formation would be used again, but under much different circumstances. Its limitations would be exposed.

Admiral Ugaki assessed the results of the battle with clarity. He was disappointed that Goto's force was unprepared and caught by surprise. Despite the defeat, Ugaki and the other members of the Japanese high command were determined to continue their efforts to retake Guadalcanal.

Though our neutralizing aerial attacks hadn't yet achieved much and the requested bombardment by army guns had not yet been carried out, four transports were slated to leave Rabaul and two from Shortland tonight. We settled the landing date as the 15th. An all-out air attack was accordingly ordered for the 13th and a night bombardment by the Third Battleship Division on the following night, thus making our resolution clear.

—12 OCTOBER 1942, FROM *FADING VICTORY: THE DIARY OF ADMIRAL MATOME UGAKI, 1941–1945* (NAVAL INSTITUTE PRESS, 2008)

Over the next two weeks, the Japanese would launch a powerful series of offensives on land, at sea, and in the air to overwhelm the American defenders of Guadalcanal.

Admiral Ugaki's Assessment of Cape Esperance

At 1040 Captain Yonajiro Hisamune and Captain Tamotsu Araki, skippers of heavy cruiser *Aoba* and heavy cruiser *Furutaka*, respectively came and I heard their reports alone. They gave me an account of the other day, saying that they were revenged for the battle off Tulagi.

Though admittedly there was a need to complete preparations for bombarding the airfield, the search conducted in advance was insufficient. When they saw several ships to the west of Savo Island coming out of a rain squall, they thought them to be our *Nissin*

and *Chitose* on transport duty and approached them. Forming a perfect letter T deployment to them, the enemy opened fire with several parachute flares. They concentrated their fires on *Aoba*, which steered her to starboard, sending repeated signals of "I am *Aoba*."

Seaman First Class Charles Olinger points out shell fragment damage to the cruiser *Boise*, photographed at the Philadelphia Navy Yard in November 1942. This damage was caused by the Japanese shell that hit the face of Turret No. 3, about 30 feet away from this spot. (National Archives)

Her fire directing tower, turrets, and bridge were disabled in a few minutes, and after firing only seven rounds of the main battery, not to speak of torpedo firing, she turned back and withdrew, extending her smoke screen. The division commander, his two staff officers, and the executive officer of the ship were killed by the same dud which fell through the front.

Furutaka was following *Aoba* at 1500 meters. Astonished by parachute flares suddenly dropped overhead, she steered to port for a while, then to starboard. An enemy shell hit a torpedo tube causing a big flame. Then the enemy rained their fire on her with this flame as a target. Number 3 turret and other torpedo tubes were disabled and a shell penetrated into the engine room. Though one of the four engines was available, the water feeding pipes of the boiler were damaged, making steam-raising impossible, and the engines finally came to a stop.

Then she listed gradually so that the ensign was pulled down and all hands ordered to abandon ship after three cheers for the emperor. The emperor's portrait was lost, as the bearer was killed. The skipper tried to commit suicide in his cabin on the bridge, but both a revolver and sword had been taken away from him. Then he went up to the bridge to tie himself to the compass, but nothing was available there. The executive officer looked after the skipper. While the skipper was ordering the executive officer to leave him, the bridge sank into the water. When he floated again, he said he was somewhere near the bow. She must have sunk from the stern.

—16 OCTOBER 1942, FROM *FADING VICTORY: THE DIARY OF ADMIRAL MATOME UGAKI, 1941–1945* (NAVAL INSTITUTE PRESS, 2008)

BREAKING THE STALEMATE

SCOTT'S VICTORY PROVIDED A VALUABLE MORALE BOOST, BUT THE NAVY was unable to control the waters off Guadalcanal. Lieutenant General Hyakutake continued to bring troops to the island, and the IJN covered these movements with massive bombardments. Two days after Scott's triumph, on the night of 13–14 October, two Japanese battleships, the *Kongō* and *Haruna*, entered the sound under the command of Vice Admiral Takeo Kurita. They bombarded Henderson Field for more than an hour, cratering the airfield and destroying more than half the available planes. Ugaki was pleased.

A wrecked F4F Wildcat, victim of a Japanese bomb or shelling. The planes at Henderson Field were vital; Navy ships and sailors fought to preserve them. In mid-October 1942 a devastating bombardment by Japanese battleships destroyed more than half the planes on the island. (National Archives)

UNITED STATES NAVAL INSTITUTE

An unprecedented attempt to bombard an airfield at night with 14-in guns attained a splendid result. The whole area of the airfield was turned into a mass conflagration of gigantic size with numerous flames shooting up. Induced explosions continued until dawn. And all this was done with no loss of our own. This proved that "if one dares to do a thing resolutely one will succeed."

—14 OCTOBER 1942, FROM *FADING VICTORY: THE DIARY OF ADMIRAL MATOME UGAKI, 1941–1945* (NAVAL INSTITUTE PRESS, 2008)

The next night, Vice Admiral Mikawa returned. His flagship the *Chōkai* and the cruiser *Kinugasa* subjected the island's defenders to another bombardment. Two escorting destroyers kept U.S. PT boats—which had started operating from Tulagi—at bay. Each of the cruisers unleashed about 400 rounds, starting fires and wrecking more valuable equipment.

These bombardments covered the approach of a high-speed reinforcement convoy. It arrived in the early hours of 15 October, and the transports started unloading at Tassafaronga. Major General Geiger was determined to attack them. Ground crews siphoned gasoline from wrecked planes while additional dive bombers arrived from Espiritu Santo. The bombers hit three of the transports: the *Azumasan Maru*, *Kyushu Maru*, and *Sasko Maru*. They were beached and became total losses. But 10,000 Japanese soldiers made it ashore. Another bombardment—this from the heavy cruisers *Maya* and *Myōkō*—took place the night of the 15th.

Admiral Nimitz's assessment of the situation was bleak: "It now appears that we are unable to control the sea in the Guadalcanal area. Thus our supply of the positions will only be done at great expense to us. The situation is not hopeless, but it is certainly critical." The situation called for decisive leadership. After a conference with his staff on the 15th, Nimitz decided to relieve Vice Admiral Ghormley and replace him with Vice Admiral William F. Halsey Jr. Admiral King approved the change. If aggressiveness was needed, Halsey was an excellent choice. He had displayed a talent for aggressive action since his early days as a destroyer captain. On 18 October Halsey relieved Ghormley and immediately began to infuse his new command with his characteristic mindset. Nimitz also sent additional reinforcements. The Army's 25th Infantry Division, based at Oahu, was ordered to the South Pacific. The carrier *Enterprise*, freshly repaired, departed Pearl Harbor on 16 October and rushed back to the area accompanied by the battleship *South Dakota* (BB-57).

Meanwhile, the campaign was moving to its climax. With the latest reinforcements, Hyakutake planned a two-pronged offensive to seize the U.S. positions. A powerful thrust, backed by large artillery, would fix American defenses along the Matanikau by frontal assault; in the meantime, Lieutenant General Maruyama would lead an assault force through the jungle and attack from the south, toward Edson's Ridge. Major General Kawaguchi was given the opportunity to lead one of the offensive thrusts and thereby redeem himself for his failure in September.

Vice Admiral William F. Halsey (left) is sworn in as Commander, South Pacific Force, by his chief of staff, Captain Miles H. Browning. This photo was taken on 17 November 1942, when Halsey already had been in command for more than a month. (National Archives)

Maruyama set out through the jungle on 15 October. Behind him, the Japanese attack across the "bloody" Matanikau slammed into Vandegrift's defenses on 20 October. Over the next three days, the Japanese pushed forward doggedly but were unable to break through. After a pause, a flanking thrust the night of the 25th managed to advance along a ridgeline but was stopped by Lieutenant Colonel Herman H. Hanneken's 2d Battalion, 7th Marines. The attack along the Matanikau failed, but it had occupied Vandegrift's attention. In concert with these assaults, Maruyama's men attacked from the south the night of the 24th. A thick rain shower covered their movements, and they broke through the initial Marine defenses. Maruyama and his staff thought they had made it through to the airfield and transmitted the good news to higher commands. It reached Admiral Ugaki.

> As I thought I could expect good news in the course of time, I went up to the weather deck and gazed at the brilliant moon of the fourteenth night. At 0135 we received an army telegram, "2100 Banzai," which meant the capture of the airfield. This settled everything. March, all forces, to enlarge the result gained! Hesitation or indecision at this moment would leave a regret forever.

—24 OCTOBER 1942, FROM *FADING VICTORY: THE DIARY OF ADMIRAL MATOME UGAKI, 1941–1945* (NAVAL INSTITUTE PRESS, 2008)

But the report was incorrect; although a penetration had occurred, the breakthrough was incomplete. A reserve battalion of the 164th Infantry moved into the breach and soldiers, together with Marines, fought back the assault at a place they named "Coffin Corner."

Anticipating victory, the IJN moved to support Maruyama's offensive with major units. Yamamoto sent powerful task forces—including four carriers and five battleships—to "apprehend and annihilate" any U.S. forces attempting to reinforce Guadalcanal. While they gathered, Mikawa sent additional troops and supplies to the island. Unaware that Henderson Field was still a threat, they arrived in daylight. A task group led by the light cruiser *Yura* swept into Ironbottom Sound the morning of the 25th. Three destroyers—the *Shiratsuyu*, *Ikazuchi*, and *Akatsuki*—chased away the destroyer-minesweepers *Trever* (DMS-16) and *Zane* (DMS-14), sank the tug *Seminole* (AT-65) and YP-284, and then bombarded the U.S. defenders. The airfield remained dormant. Heavy rains had turned it into a muddy quagmire, but as the sun dried it out, Cactus came to life. The *Yura* was hit by two bombs, flooding her after engine room. She limped away, but a patrolling B-17 hit her again that afternoon, and she had to be scuttled.

That night, the Japanese attacked again. General Kawaguchi's force, which had lost time trekking through the jungle, augmented Maruyama's assault. The soldiers and Marines stopped them at Coffin Corner. The defeated Japanese survivors withdrew back into the jungle.

Anticipating that powerful naval forces would support the Japanese land offensive, Halsey boldly sent his two carriers—the *Hornet* and *Enterprise*—north of the Santa Cruz Islands, hoping to position them for

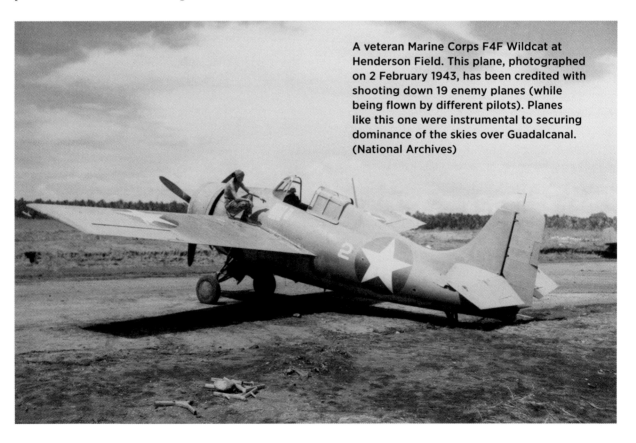

A veteran Marine Corps F4F Wildcat at Henderson Field. This plane, photographed on 2 February 1943, has been credited with shooting down 19 enemy planes (while being flown by different pilots). Planes like this one were instrumental to securing dominance of the skies over Guadalcanal. (National Archives)

an ambush. As he explained to Admiral Nimitz, "I had to begin throwing punches almost immediately." While the carriers raced to rendezvous, Vandegrift flew to Nouméa to meet the new theater commander. Halsey asked Vandegrift if he could hold. The Marine general responded that he could, but he needed more support. Halsey closed the meeting promising to give him "everything I have."

Rear Admiral Thomas C. Kinkaid pictured on board his flagship, the carrier *Enterprise*, on 22 July 1942. Kinkaid commanded the Navy's carrier task forces at the Battle of the Santa Cruz Islands. (National Archives)

THE BATTLE OF THE SANTA CRUZ ISLANDS

On the morning of 25 October, Vice Admiral Kondo's Advance Force was racing toward Guadalcanal, eager to exploit Maruyama's "victory." To the east, Vice Admiral Nagumo's carrier force, with the *Shōkaku*, *Zuikaku*, and light carrier *Zuihō*, was ready to ambush any U.S. forces that appeared. About 60 miles ahead of his carriers, Nagumo positioned Rear Admiral Hiroaki Abe's Vanguard Group, with the battleships *Hiei* and *Kirishima*. They would scout with their floatplanes but not find Halsey's carriers, now commanded by Rear Admiral Thomas C. Kinkaid. Later that day, the Japanese admirals learned that Maruyama's victory declaration was premature. Kondō sent a strike from the carrier *Junyō* to harass the enemy installations at Lunga Point.

American searches were more effective. A B-17 found Kondō's force, and a PBY sighted Abe's vanguard. Another PBY flown by Lieutenant (junior grade) Robert J. Lampshire located all three of Nagumo's carriers. Word of Lampshire's sighting reached the *Enterprise* at 1150 that morning. Kinkaid assessed the situation; the Japanese were out of range, but if they continued to close, an afternoon strike was possible. He decided to launch 12 armed Dauntlesses in a search; a strike from the *Enterprise* would follow and attack what the searchers found. Nagumo and Abe, aware they had been sighted, turned north. Kinkaid's search and strike found nothing.

Abe and Nagumo reversed course that night and headed south again. Radar-equipped PBYs—"Black Cats"—prowled north of San Cristobal and found them. Abe's vanguard dodged a torpedo attack. A lone PBY bombing run narrowly missed the carrier *Zuikaku*. Fearing he was heading into a trap, Nagumo reversed course before sunrise. Kinkaid failed to receive word of these sightings until after the morning search was airborne. Some of his staff urged him to attack, but he held back, waiting for more definitive information. Scouting Dauntlesses located and attacked Abe's ships just before 0630, but they did no damage. Less than 30 minutes later, another group of search planes found Nagumo's carriers, just 200 miles away from Kinkaid's TF 61. Kinkaid launched a powerful strike from both carriers; a second strike from the *Hornet* took off as soon as the planes could be spotted.

In the meantime, Japanese search planes had found TF 61. Nagumo knew he was facing at least one U.S. carrier by 0700. Wary of being attacked with armed planes on board—as he had been at Midway—he launched his first strike immediately. Fifty-three planes from the *Shōkaku* and *Zuikaku* formed the first strike;

unlike their U.S. counterparts, the Japanese planes formed into a cohesive unit as they set out. Ten planes from the *Zuihō* joined them.

The Americans struck first; two scouting Dauntlesses checked their sector, and, finding it empty, set out to find Nagumo's carriers. At 0740, they hit the *Zuihō* with a 500-pound bomb, tearing open a large hole in the flight deck and preventing her from recovering aircraft. The unexpected attack added to Nagumo's fears; he sent his second strike from the *Shōkaku* immediately, without waiting for the planes from the *Zuikaku*. Her planes would follow independently. Kondō headed northeast to support Nagumo. Abe set a course for the U.S. carriers, looking for an opportunity to bring his battleship guns to bear.

Shortly after 0900, the Dauntlesses of the *Hornet's* first strike group found Nagumo. The dive bombers attacked the *Shōkaku* from the south, while the *Zuikaku* remained hidden behind a rain squall. The first bombs missed, but three or four slammed into the carrier, shattering her flight deck and putting a stop to all flight operations. Fires burned out of control for the next five

hours, but the *Kidō Butai* veteran survived. The failure to deliver a coordinated strike prevented further damage to Nagumo's carriers. The TBF Avenger torpedo planes in the *Hornet's* first wave focused their attacks on Abe's Vanguard Group. The *Enterprise's* strike and *Hornet's* second strike did the same. Dive bombers scored a series of hits on the cruiser *Chikuma*, wrecking her bridge, starting fires on the aft deck, and reducing her speed. She limped away to the north. The distributed Japanese formations worked as intended, drawing aerial attacks away from the fragile carriers.

In the meantime, the first Japanese strike—a cohesive mass of attack aircraft and escorting fighters—was hitting TF 61. Kate torpedo bombers divided into two groups to attack the *Hornet* from both bows while Vals gently descended to their pushover point. Wildcats were vectored to intercept. They broke up some of the attacking formations, but three bombs hit the carrier. Two penetrated deep into the ship before exploding; the third burst on the edge of the flight deck aft, creating a large hole. Two torpedoes hit the starboard side. The *Hornet* lost power and slowly came to a stop. Another wave of

The damaged carrier *Hornet* is dead in the water during the Battle of the Santa Cruz Islands. She is just beyond the plane's wingtip. Ahead of her, the cruiser *Northampton* is attempting to take her in tow. Other cruisers, including the *Pensacola* (just above the tip of the wing), circle around the wounded carrier. The one in the foreground is either the *San Diego* or *Juneau*. Her aft turrets are trained on the photographing plane. (National Archives)

Vals bore in; one slammed into the carrier's bridge before crashing through the flight deck. A damaged straggler appeared as the attack was winding down.

> Courageously fighting his faltering controls, the Japanese pulled out over her [the *Hornet*'s] starboard bow and reversed course over the *Northampton* in "a lazy glide" back toward the *Hornet*. Despite every gun that could bear, he crossed ahead of her bow, banked sharply, and sliced through the hull just ahead of the port forward gun gallery. The burning fuselage slanted down through the gallery deck into the forward elevator pit, where it ignited a nasty fire.
>
> —JOHN B. LUNDSTROM, *THE FIRST TEAM AND THE GUADALCANAL CAMPAIGN* (NAVAL INSTITUTE PRESS, 1994)

The well-executed attack left the *Hornet* crippled, but of 53 Japanese planes from the first strike, only 15 would return. The offensive pulse was powerful, but fragile. More pulses were coming. A third strike, 29 planes from the *Junyō*, launched soon after 0900.

The first group of the second Japanese strike, the *Shōkaku*'s dive bombers, arrived over the U.S. task forces about an hour later. They lined up for attacks on the *Enterprise*. Escorting Wildcats and antiaircraft fire knocked down some of the attackers, but three bombs damaged the carrier in quick succession. One punched through the flight deck forward and exploded just outside the hull; another struck amidships and detonated deep inside the ship; and the third was a near miss just off the starboard quarter. It exploded in the water and opened seams in the hull plates. Despite this damage, the *Enterprise* resumed flight operations relatively quickly. The second group of the second strike arrived soon after; Kates from *Zuikaku* attacked the *Enterprise* from two directions. Intercepting Wildcats broke up their timing. One crippled Kate crashed into the forward guns of the destroyer *Smith* (DD-378), starting a terrible fire. Others reached the launch point, but radical maneuvers allowed the carrier to comb the approaching torpedo tracks.

While the damaged *Enterprise* struggled to make repairs and rearm fighters, the *Junyō*'s Vals appeared at 1115. The first group attacked the carrier in shallow dives. Antiaircraft fire spoiled their aim. A second

The carrier *Enterprise* under attack by Japanese bombers on 26 October 1942. A bomb has just exploded in the water off the port side. Note the smoke streaming from her forward section below the flight deck and the numerous antiaircraft shell bursts in the sky. (National Archives)

group attacked the *South Dakota*, hitting her forward turret. A third group attacked the light cruiser *San Juan*. A bomb sliced through her stern and detonated beneath the ship, causing her to lose steering control for several minutes.

With the *Enterprise* damaged and the *Hornet* crippled, Kinkaid decided to withdraw. Attempts to tow the *Hornet* away from danger were interrupted by Kates from the *Junyō*. One of their torpedoes hit the carrier's starboard side, increasing her list to 14 degrees. A third strike from the *Zuikaku* arrived a few minutes later; they scored near misses that increased the list. The *Hornet* was abandoned. Attempts to scuttle her with destroyer guns and torpedoes failed, and her burning hulk was still afloat when Japanese destroyers of Kondō's support force found her that night. The carrier finally sank in the early hours of 27 October.

The Battle of the Santa Cruz Islands was over. Although the *Enterprise* was the Navy's last operational carrier in the Pacific, most of her air crew, and most of the *Hornet*'s, had survived. Nagumo had not been so fortunate. Half of the Japanese carrier aircraft had been lost in the battle. Forty-nine percent of the Val pilots and 39 percent of the Kate pilots had been killed. Twenty-three section leaders (or officers of higher rank) were killed or missing. The Japanese air crews had been devastated, a more significant loss than the severe damage to the *Shōkaku* and *Zuihō*. Halsey, recognizing that a major enemy effort had been thwarted, resolved to take the offensive.

HALSEY MOVES AGGRESSIVELY

Although the soldiers and Marines on Guadalcanal successfully defended their perimeter against a series of determined attacks, the Japanese were unwilling to accept defeat. They resolved to make another attempt, in November. Admiral Yamamoto crafted a plan designed to guarantee victory. Simultaneously, Halsey accelerated the shipment of supplies to the island so that Vandegrift could end Japanese resistance and bring the campaign to a successful conclusion. These two plans would collide in mid-November and decide the campaign.

Between 23 October and 11 November, 65 destroyer transport sorties and two cruiser loads

Climax in the South Pacific

The enemy had suffered severe casualties in the unsuccessful assaults on our lines during the last days of October. Without allowing time for enemy replacement of losses by fresh reinforcements, we launched a counter-attack. Beginning about 0030, 30 October, *Atlanta* and 4 destroyers bombarded the Japanese positions back of Point Cruz for eight hours. At dawn the following morning, the 5th Marines struck across the Matanikau River supported by heavy air bombing and strafing and occasional bombardment by available surface forces. By 3 November they had advanced beyond Point Cruz, killing many of the enemy and capturing much equipment.

On the preceding night, 2–3 November, however, Japanese cruisers and destroyers had landed about 1500 troops with artillery east of Koli Point. Our offensive to the westward was checked to counter this new threat which was fortunately smaller than the enemy had planned. Apprehensive over the presence of our strong surface forces near Guadalcanal, they hesitated to bring in combat loaded APs [transports] with additional troops and were therefore unable to make the general attack from all sides planned for 3 November.

On 4 November *San Francisco*, *Helena*, and *Sterett* bombarded this new force east of Koli Point, setting many fires and destroying stores and ammunition. After several days of fighting, many of the enemy remaining near Koli Point were surrounded at Tetere and from 9–11 November annihilated.

Despite our successes in the skirmishes on Guadalcanal, the situation appeared critical. Our only available carrier was the incompletely repaired *Enterprise*, not expected to be fully ready for action until 21 November. *Saratoga* was just leaving Pearl Harbor following repairs and extensive improvements in A.A. armament after being torpedoed by a submarine on 31 August. It is possible we had superiority in numbers on Guadalcanal but the Japanese were continually landing fresh troops and massing a large assault force to the north. The October battles had achieved some reduction in Japanese warships, but the fleet gathered against us was still far stronger than our available fleet. We were inferior in land-based as well as carrier aircraft. On 10 November when it became apparent that the Japanese were on the eve of renewing the grand scale attack on Guadalcanal, the situation did not look promising.

—*SOLOMONS ISLANDS CAMPAIGN—BATTLE OF THE SOLOMONS, 11–15 NOVEMBER 1942*, REAR ADMIRAL R. A. SPRUANCE, DEPUTY COMMANDER, PACIFIC FLEET

had brought a large contingent of the Japanese 38th (Nagoya) Infantry Division to Guadalcanal, increasing the total number of Japanese troops on the island from 22,000 to 30,000. The remainder of the 38th Division, including its artillery and other vital supplies would be brought in a large convoy. Once it arrived, the Japanese expected to finally push the Americans off the island.

Halsey traveled to Espiritu Santo and Guadalcanal to personally assess the situation and guide his own offensive moves. On 7 November, he met with Rear Admiral Fitch at Espiritu Santo. The South Pacific air commander thought it was a good time to be aggressive. He had good numbers of reserve aircraft and a large contingent of fighters and dive bombers based at Guadalcanal. The next morning, Halsey proceeded to Guadalcanal to meet with General Vandegrift. The general described the visit as "a wonderful breath of fresh air" that improved morale. Halsey conferred with Major General Geiger and Brigadier General Louis E. Woods, his chief of staff. Halsey ordered Woods to relieve Geiger as Cactus Air Force commander, so that Geiger could work with Fitch at Espiritu Santo to coordinate the growing number of Marine aircraft in the theater. On the 9th, Halsey departed Guadalcanal; he arrived back at his headquarters in Nouméa the next day and was greeted by an intelligence analysis from Admiral Nimitz. It provided a clear estimate of Japanese intentions:

a. Daily air attacks on Guadalcanal, beginning 10 November.

b. Transports to leave Shortlands on the evening of 11 November.

c. Bombardment of Henderson Field during the night of 11–12 November.

d. Concentrated air attack on Henderson Field on 12 November.

e. Landing in division strength the night of 12–13 November.

It was clear a large offensive was coming. Nimitz closed with a comment that spoke to his faith in Halsey and his men: "While this looks like a big punch, I am confident that you with your forces will take their measure." Halsey had already dispatched three separate forces toward Guadalcanal. TF 67, under the command of Rear Admiral Turner, contained two of them. The reinforcement group, with Turner commanding from the transport McCawley (APA-4), left Nouméa on 8 November. The four transports McCawley, Crescent City (APA-21), President Adams (APA-19), and President Jackson (APA-18)—known as the "Unholy Four"—carried the Army's 182nd Regiment, the 4th Marine Replacement Battalion, and Naval Defense Force personnel. Blessed so far by good fortune, the four transports had survived the initial landings and several resupply runs. For this voyage, they were escorted by the cruisers Portland (CA-33) and Juneau (CL-52) and the destroyers Barton (DD-599), Monssen (DD-436), and O'Bannon (DD-450). Turner's second group was his covering force, Task Group [TG] 67.4, under the command of Rear Admiral Daniel J. Callaghan. Callaghan had been Ghormley's chief of staff; as a task group commander, Callaghan flew his flag in the cruiser San Francisco. He had been her captain before the war, and the crew knew him as "Uncle Dan."

Callaghan also had the cruisers Pensacola (CA-24) and Helena, along with the destroyers Cushing (DD-376), Laffey, Sterett (DD-407), Gwin (DD-433), Preston (DD-379), and Buchanan. His screen commander was

Daniel J. Callaghan photographed as a captain while commanding the cruiser San Francisco in 1941. As a rear admiral he would lead a hastily formed task force against a superior Japanese formation the night of 12–13 November 1942. (National Archives)

Commander Thomas M. Stokes, leader of Destroyer Division 10, on board the *Cushing*. They left Espiritu Santo on 10 November and rendezvoused with Turner southeast of San Cristobal early on the morning of the 11th. The destroyer *Shaw* (DD-373) had joined the screen the previous day, giving the force a total of five cruisers and ten destroyers.

That same morning, the third group, TG 62.4 under Rear Admiral Norman Scott, was arriving off Lunga Point. Scott, in the cruiser *Atlanta* (CL-51) and with the destroyers *Aaron Ward*, *Fletcher* (DD-445), *Lardner* (DD-478), and *McCalla*, had escorted three attack cargo ships, the *Betelgeuse* (AKA-11), *Libra* (AKA-12), and *Zeilin* (APA-3). They left Espiritu Santo the day before Callaghan and brought the 1st Marine Aviation Engineer Battalion, Marine Air Wing 1 ground personnel, Marine replacements, and supplies. Captain Tobin, commander of Destroyer Squadron 12, was on board the *Aaron Ward* and commanded Scott's screen.

With his transports on their way to Guadalcanal, Halsey considered how he could thwart Japanese intentions. His most powerful striking group was Kinkaid's TF 16, with the carrier *Enterprise* and the battleships *Washington* and *South Dakota*. Halsey summoned Kinkaid on the evening of 10 November and the two discussed their options. It was important to preserve the *Enterprise*. Halsey ordered Callaghan to dispatch the *Pensacola* and two destroyers to augment TF 16's screen. At 1100 the next morning, Kinkaid sailed from Nouméa with orders to arrive 200 miles south of San Cristobal by 0800 on 13 November, ready to strike Japanese forces in or near Guadalcanal. Halsey expected TF 16 to be able to counter Japanese moves; if necessary, he would detach the two battleships and four escorting destroyers under Rear Admiral Willis A. Lee. He could strike any Japanese forces that made it past Callaghan and Scott.

PREPARING FOR THE FINAL BATTLE

Admiral Yamamoto also coordinated the movements of distributed task forces. The reinforcement group, under Rear Admiral Tanaka, would ferry the remainder of the 38th Infantry Division to Guadalcanal on board 11 high-speed transports. Eleven destroyers would provide escort. The ships assembled in the Shortlands on 12 November and left that evening for Guadalcanal. The Volunteer Attack Force, commanded by newly promoted Vice Admiral Abe, preceded them. Abe flew his flag in the battleship *Hiei*, the most capable of the Japanese fast battleships. Relegated to training duty by the London Treaty of 1930, she had been modernized and used as a prototype for the advanced fire control systems fitted to the super-battleships *Yamato* and *Musashi*. Together with the battleship *Kirishima*, the *Hiei* would bombard Henderson Field the night of 12 November and render it unserviceable, freeing the way for Tanaka's approach. Rear Admiral Susumu Kimura's Destroyer Squadron 10, with the light cruiser *Nagara* and six destroyers, screened Abe's battleships. Captain Yasuhide Setoyama's three destroyers augmented the screen and were given the mission of intercepting any U.S. PT boats. Five more destroyers—Destroyer Squadron 4, under Rear Admiral Tamotsu Takama—joined Abe in the afternoon; Takama would sweep the sound ahead of the rest of the formation.

Abe's Volunteer Attack Force was subordinate to Vice Admiral Kondo's Advanced Force. Kondō departed Truk on 9 November and operated from a position north of Santa Isabel. He flew his flag in the heavy cruiser *Atago*. Like Abe, he had two fast battleships, the *Kongō* and *Haruna*. The light carrier *Junyō* and aircraft cruiser *Tone* provided air cover. The heavy cruiser *Takao*, the light cruiser *Sendai*, and five escorting destroyers rounded out Kondō's formation.

The final Japanese force was an additional bombardment group commanded by Vice Admiral Mikawa. Mikawa had four heavy cruisers, two light cruisers, and six destroyers. He planned to depart the Shortlands the morning of 13 November, so that he could arrive off Henderson Field that night. He would destroy anything Abe's bombardment the night before had missed.

Yamamoto expected these four task forces to destroy the airfield, prevent U.S. planes from interfering with the approach of the transports, and land sufficient troops to seize the island. He supported their movements with a series of air raids from Rabaul and a newly constructed airfield at Buin on Bougainville. The first of these struck on the morning of the 11th, as Scott's attack transports were unloading. Accurate fire from the *Atlanta* and the other escorts prevented any hits, but three near misses flooded one of the *Zeilin*'s holds. A second strike arrived later that day and focused on the Cactus airfields.

That evening, Scott's transports withdrew, and his warships joined up with Callaghan's TG 67.4. Turner's "Unholy Four" arrived before dawn on the 12th and

The Japanese air attack of 12 November 1942. In the foreground, the *President Jackson* maneuvers to avoid attacking planes. In the distance, smoke rises from the cruiser *San Francisco*; a Japanese Betty has just crashed into her after superstructure. Note the numerous bursts in the sky from antiaircraft shells. (National Archives)

started unloading. The destroyers *Buchanan* and *Cushing* bombarded Japanese supply dumps near Tassafaronga Point, setting ammunition and fuel ablaze.

Around 1400 that afternoon, a flight of Bettys and escorting Zeros from Rabaul attacked. Turner was warned of their approach by Paul Mason, an Allied coastwatcher at Buin. The Bettys came in out of the clouds at 500 feet and were jumped by patrolling Wildcats. As the attackers closed, antiaircraft guns on board the ships opened up; few of the Bettys got close enough to release their torpedoes, but one closed on the *San Francisco*.

Every gun that would bear was firing on the plane as it approached the *San Francisco* from nearly astern. The cockpit was engulfed in flames and the plane was nearly out of control, its left wing tilted at a forty-five-degree angle. On the after machine gun platform, James Meacham (S2c) could see that the plane was about to land directly in his lap. Still the gunners on the four twenty-millimeter mounts poured their fire into the plane as it grew larger and larger in their sights. At the last instant, Meacham tore off

the JL phones he was wearing, wrapped his face in a life jacket, and jumped to the boat deck below as the platform exploded.

—JAMES W. GRACE, *THE NAVAL BATTLE OF GUADALCANAL* (NAVAL INSTITUTE PRESS, 1999)

The plane glanced off the ship and fell into the water, but its ruptured fuel tanks doused the after superstructure in high-octane gasoline. The fires wrecked the after conning station, destroyed the aft fire control positions for the main and secondary guns, and killed 15 men. Fourteen others were wounded, including Commander Marc H. Crouter, the ship's executive officer.

Most of the attacking aircraft had been destroyed, causing Vice Admiral Jinichi Kusaka, who arrived at Rabaul in late September to assume command of the IJN's 11th Air Fleet, to question the effectiveness of these strikes. He would not send any more for the next two days, when the situation was most critical. In the meantime, B-17s searching from Espiritu Santo sighted Abe's bombardment force. Turner correctly assessed that these ships were planning to bombard Henderson Field and resolved to stop them.

FRIDAY THE 13TH

VICE ADMIRAL ABE'S APPROACH CAUGHT THE AMERICANS OFF GUARD.
Kinkaid's TF 16 was too far away to intervene, and Turner had planned to
withdraw TF 67 that evening. Turner knew he had to thwart the bombardment.
He took the "Unholy Four" and three destroyers back to Espiritu Santo and
ordered Callaghan to take the remaining warships and "return to Cactus
tonight and strike enemy ships present." Callaghan and Scott would try to
ambush Abe. They had just five cruisers and eight destroyers against two
battleships and a powerful force of screening vessels.

The destroyer *Aaron Ward*, photographed approaching the carrier *Wasp* on 17 August 1942. The *Aaron Ward* was the flagship of Captain Robert G. Tobin and lead ship of Callaghan's rear destroyers during the First Naval Battle of Guadalcanal. Note her FD radar above the main battery director and Measure 12 (modified) camouflage scheme. (National Archives)

Abe was apprehensive about the bombardment. He had been shaken by the death of his friend Rear Admiral Gotō the month before. Survivors of Cape Esperance had told Abe that the Americans had surprised Gotō and that he "had died believing he was the victim of friendly gunfire." Despite his nervousness, Abe failed to anticipate Turner's resolve and did not expect to meet serious opposition in Ironbottom Sound. Admiral Ugaki was not nearly so sanguine. After Turner's force was sighted, he urged the Combined Fleet staff to provide more substantial covering forces for the bombardment, but they believed "a destroyer squadron in the van would be enough" and "the enemy would withdraw by nightfall."

Callaghan entered the sound fully aware his small force was the only thing preventing a repeat of the devastating bombardment in mid-October. He and his crews were tired. Aerial attacks, submarine alerts, and the sweep the night before had kept them at general quarters half of the time since they left port. As the admiral thought through how best to approach the upcoming battle, the weather worsened. "Frequent, intense lighting" was observed, and a storm moved through the area, reducing visibility significantly.

CALLAGHAN'S PLAN

Since it had been effective at Cape Esperance, Callaghan adopted Scott's linear formation; he placed his cruisers in the center and destroyers at either end of the line. In action reports it was referred to as "Battle Formation B-1." Four destroyers were in the van: the *Cushing*, *Laffey*, *Sterett*, and *O'Bannon*. They were followed by the light cruiser *Atlanta* and then the larger cruisers: the *San Francisco*, *Portland*, and *Helena*. The light cruiser *Juneau* was behind them, followed by the last four destroyers: *Aaron Ward*, *Barton*, *Monssen*, and *Fletcher*. The van destroyers were led by Commander Stokes and the rear group by Captain Tobin. Neither

of them was well-equipped to coordinate their ships at night. Among the destroyers, only the *Fletcher* and *O'Bannon* had SG radars. Callaghan was not much better off; like Scott, he selected the *San Francisco* as his flagship because of her effective facilities, but she still lacked SG radar.

Lieutenant (junior grade) John E. Bennett's observations provide a window into Callaghan's mindset. Bennett alternated as officer of the deck with Lieutenant Commander Bruce McCandless on board the *San Francisco*. On the evening of 12 November, as Callaghan's TG 67.4 returned to Guadalcanal, Bennett overheard the admiral conversing with Captain Cassin Young on the starboard wing of the navigation bridge.

> They were discussing the unannounced fact that there were battleships . . . coming . . . that night and that our little group of cruisers and destroyers were ordered to prevent them at all costs from bombarding Henderson Field and landing reinforcements from the accompanying transports. . . . Captain Cassin Young . . . was in an understandably agitated state, sometimes waving his arms, as he remarked, "but this is suicide." Admiral Dan Callaghan replied, "Yes I know, but we have to do it."
>
> —CAPTAIN J. E. BENNETT, USN (RET.), "CALLAGHAN WAS CALM AND COLLECTED AT GUADALCANAL," *SHIPMATE* (APRIL 1996)

Callaghan was resolved to thwart the Japanese bombardment and had worked out a way to do it. He knew that under the right circumstances, he could overpower one of the Japanese battleships. The Naval War College's fighting strength comparisons showed that, when the ranges were close—less than 10,000 yards—two U.S. cruisers had an advantage over one of Abe's battleships. With three of them, Callaghan would have a decisive advantage, provided he could bring them close enough. Understandably, this desperate plan agitated Captain Young. No matter how feasible the idea might have been in theory, cruisers were not likely to survive close range action with battleships. It is likely that,

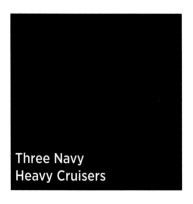

Three Navy Heavy Cruisers

Two Navy Heavy Cruisers

One Japanese Battleship

Relative fighting strengths at 8,000 yards as estimated by the Naval War College. Callaghan would have been aware of these ratios and they likely informed his plans.

after Young's reaction, Callaghan resolved to keep the details of his plan to himself. He would coordinate the actions of his cruisers in battle from the bridge of the *San Francisco*, using the TBS radio to communicate orders at critical moments and bring his cruisers to decisive range. The other ships of the formation would be left to the leadership of Scott, Stokes, and Tobin. Without a plan to guide them, they would fall back on the tactical heuristics developed before the war: aggressive action, effective gunfire, and individual initiative.

MAKING CONTACT

Vice Admiral Abe neared Savo Sound in an approach disposition designed to protect his battleships. The five destroyers of Rear Admiral Takama's Destroyer Squadron 4 were in the van, 5,000 yards ahead of the main body. Behind Takama was the light cruiser *Nagara*; the battleships *Hiei* and *Kirishima* followed in her wake. Spread out at an angle to either side were the six destroyers of Destroyer Squadron 10. Commander Tameichi Hara captained the *Amatsukaze*, the middle destroyer on the left flank, and was concerned about the complexity of the formation: "Nerves tightened in *Amatsukaze* as we waited expectantly for orders to slow down and change to a less complex formation. No such orders came."

As they neared their objective, the weather worsened. Officers watched for signal lights on Guadalcanal as they headed south-southwest past Savo Island. The lights would help them navigate through the narrow entrance to the sound, but they missed them. Abe realized they were too far south and broke radio silence to order a reversal of course. The maneuver disrupted the complex formation. Takama's five destroyers missed the order and turned late; they advanced along the starboard quarter of the formation to regain their position. Three of them—the *Samidare*, *Murasame*, and Takama's flagship, the *Asagumo*—crossed behind the *Kirishima* and made their way around to port. When Abe's group entered Savo Sound, they were out of place. Only the two others, the *Yūdachi* and *Harusame*, had returned to the van. As Abe approached TG 67.4, his screen was disorganized. Fortunately, the weather had cleared, and the signal lights were visible. The battleships' guns were loaded in preparation for the bombardment.

Callaghan's long line of ships paralleled the north coast of Guadalcanal at 15 knots, keeping within one or two miles of the shoreline. At about 0118, as they approached Lunga Point, the van destroyers sighted one of the Japanese lights on the shore at Tassafaronga. Callaghan suspected it meant Abe's force was approaching. At about 0124, he increased speed to 18 knots.

The *Helena*'s SG radar once again found the Japanese first; Captain Hoover reported the contact over TBS at about 0126 as "two contacts, bearing 310 degrees,

---

Order of Battle: 12–13 November 1942

Navy Forces - Rear Admiral Daniel J. Callaghan

Van Destroyers
 Cushing (Commander Thomas M. Stokes)
 Laffey
 Sterett
 O'Bannon

Cruisers
 Atlanta (Rear Admiral Norman Scott)
 San Francisco (flag)
 Portland
 Helena
 Juneau

Rear Destroyers
 Aaron Ward (Captain Robert G. Tobin)
 Barton
 Monssen
 Fletcher

IJN Forces - Vice Admiral Hiroaki Abe

Bombardment Unit
 Hiei (flag)
 Kirishima

Destroyer Squadron 10
 Nagara (Rear Admiral Susumu Kimura)
 Akatsuki
 Inazuma
 Ikazuchi
 Yukikaze
 Amatsukaze
 Teruzuki

Destroyer Squadron 4
 Asagumo (Rear Admiral Tamotsu Takama)
 Murasame
 Samidare
 Yūdachi
 Harusame

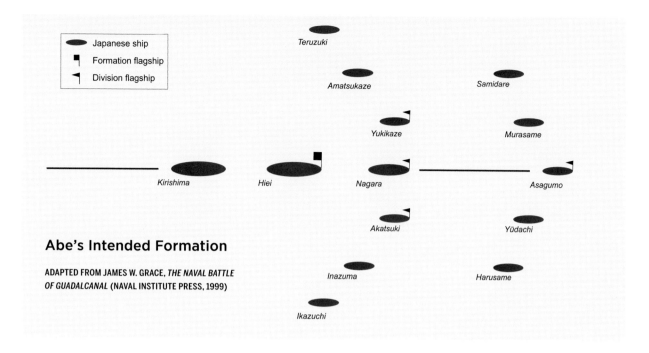

Abe's Intended Formation

ADAPTED FROM JAMES W. GRACE, *THE NAVAL BATTLE OF GUADALCANAL* (NAVAL INSTITUTE PRESS, 1999)

Legend:
- Japanese ship
- Formation flagship
- Division flagship

Teruzuki
Amatsukaze
Samidare
Yukikaze
Murasame
Kirishima
Hiei
Nagara
Asagumo
Akatsuki
Yūdachi
Inazuma
Harusame
Ikazuchi

distance 31,900 yards." The unprecedented detection range convinced Lieutenant Gash, the radar officer, that he was tracking a battleship. Callaghan tried to make sense of the developing situation; Hoover's report was sparse and lacked the contact's speed and heading, but it gave a clear bearing. Callaghan immediately ordered a course change to intercept. The van came around to 310 and the other ships followed. At 0132, Hoover updated his contact report: "Now three contacts, bearing 312 degrees, distance 26,000 yards." A follow-up transmission gave the enemy course as 105 degrees and speed as approximately 23 knots. The formations were closing each other at nearly a mile a minute.

At 0135, Callaghan ordered his column to change course to 000 and queried the van destroyers, "Any of you boys have her up there?" The initial response was negative. The SC radars on board the *Cushing*, *Laffey*, and *Sterett* had been unable to detect the Japanese against the background of Savo Island. The *O'Bannon*, with her SG, had better luck. She responded that she had a contact on a relative bearing of 45 degrees. Callaghan asked for the range. Commander Edwin R. Wilkinson indicated just 7,000 yards, significantly closer than Callaghan was expecting.

Callaghan warned his formation contact was imminent: "Three unidentified ships on our port bow, bearing approximately 45 to 60 degrees. Be on the alert." About a minute later, at 0139, the *Helena* reported again: "We have four in a line." Callaghan asked for the range. Hoover responded that the contact was just 3,400 yards from the van destroyers. Commander Stokes on board

The destroyer *Cushing*, lead ship of Rear Admiral Callaghan's column and flagship of Commander Thomas M. Stokes, commander of Destroyer Division 10. She is pictured off the Mare Island Navy Yard on 15 July 1942. (Naval History and Heritage Command)

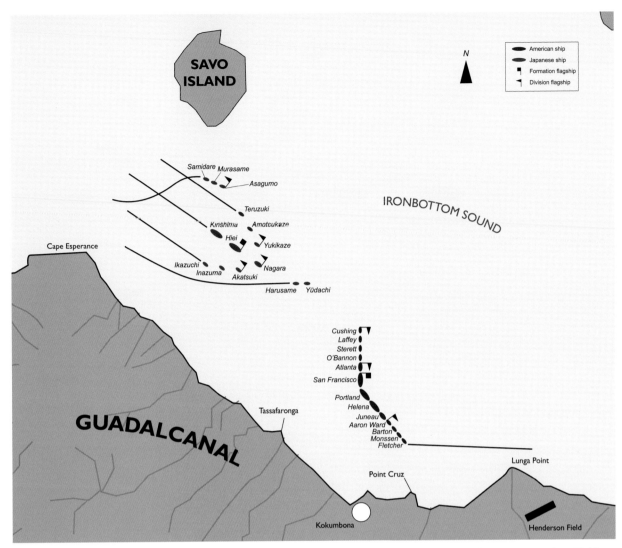

SAVO ISLAND

IRONBOTTOM SOUND

	American ship
	Japanese ship
	Formation flagship
	Division flagship

N

Samidare Murasame
Asagumo

Teruzuki

Kirishima   Amatsukaze
Hiei   Yukikaze

Cape Esperance

Ikazuchi   Nagara
Inazuma   Akatsuki

Harusame   Yūdachi

Cushing
Laffey
Sterett
O'Bannon
Atlanta
San Francisco

Portland
Helena
Juneau
Aaron Ward
Barton
Monssen
Fletcher

Tassafaronga

GUADALCANAL

Lunga Point

Point Cruz

Kokumbona

Henderson Field

Relative positions of the approaching formations before contact was made the night of 12–13 November 1942.

The destroyer *Laffey*, pictured at Espiritu Santo in September 1942. Her decks are crowded with survivors from the carrier *Wasp*, which had just been sunk. The cruiser in the distance is the *Helena*. The *Laffey* was crippled, torpedoed, and set afire during the First Naval Battle of Guadalcanal. Her captain, Lieutenant Commander William E. Hank, ordered her abandoned shortly before she rolled over and sank. (Naval History and Heritage Command)

UNITED STATES NAVAL INSTITUTE

the *Cushing* sighted them: "Looks like ships dead ahead on port bow." These were the *Yūdachi* and *Harusame*. Again, Callaghan asked for the range. Stokes responded, "Ship crossing from port to starboard, range 4,000 yards, maximum." A minute later, Callaghan asked, "What do you make of it now?" Hoover responded that the *Helena* had "a total of about ten targets." Stokes asked permission to fire torpedoes, and Callaghan told him to do so. As the *Cushing* swung to port to unmask her torpedo battery, the van was thrown into confusion. The van destroyers started a disjointed turn, coming to a course of approximately 310. The *Atlanta* turned left to avoid them.

Abe had less information than Callaghan. The *Yūdachi* and *Harusame* had sighted the *Cushing* and broadcast a warning, but Abe was uncertain where they were and how close the American ships had come. His confusion quickly changed to surprise when the sharp eyes of one of his staff officers sighted the lead ships of Callaghan's formation. He resolved to act before they could open fire.

At 0144, Callaghan asked again, "What do you make of it?" Hoover indicated that the enemy formation appeared to be a cruising disposition, with the heavy ships in the center surrounded by a circular screen, an accurate judgement of Abe's now compressed formation. Callaghan asked for an updated bearing and Stokes reported that the nearest targets bore 60 degrees from the last course ordered. Callaghan asked Hoover for more details; did he still have targets to port? Yes. Callaghan immediately recognized that the Japanese had not slipped past him. He announced to his formation, "Enemy is on our starboard bow and there are also ships to port. Stand by to open fire." He ordered the *San Francisco* to come left to course 280, to unmask the guns of his cruisers.

Before his flagship could come to the new course, Callaghan noticed that the *Atlanta* was out of position. "What are you doing?" he asked her commanding officer, Captain Samuel P. Jenkins. "Avoiding own destroyers," Jenkins replied. Callaghan ordered Stokes to come back to course 000; the admiral was sending his four van destroyers, along with the *Atlanta*, through the enemy formation where they could seek targets of opportunity for their torpedoes. Callaghan's decision to send his destroyers ahead while his cruisers turned adhered to prewar tactics. The "V" formation for night search and attack, developed and practiced before the war, was designed to allow destroyers to penetrate an enemy disposition while following cruisers broke off and supported their efforts with gunfire. Callaghan had practiced it. His orders suggest he was improvising a similar approach.

It was now about 0146. With the enemy all around, Callaghan ordered his ships to open fire: "Odd ships commence fire to starboard, even to port." He wanted to make sure that fire was evenly distributed among the available targets, but the order was poorly conceived. Practically all his ships had already identified a target and were ready to open fire. Several of them abandoned these targets to find new ones, wasting valuable seconds. While gun directors and turrets slewed to new targets, Japanese searchlights penetrated the darkness. One from the *Akatsuki* traversed the U.S. column and came to rest on the *Atlanta*. Several more flashed out from the *Hiei*'s superstructure; one fixed on the *Helena*. The night exploded as both sides opened fire.

The *Sterett* Approaches the Enemy

"Solution!" [Edward F.] Chapman called out. "Enemy course 107—speed 23 knots." I relayed the solution to the bridge, where the skipper and Tom McWhorter needed all the information we could provide. Meanwhile, an unidentified voice on the TBS announced that there was a second enemy force to the right of the first one. We continued to head right for them, and I wondered why the first four destroyers did not break away from the cruisers to conduct a torpedo attack since we had the exclusive advantage of radar. Still there was no order from the OTC to do anything but move right down the middle, between the two Japanese forces. The range closed at an astonishing rate. When we were within four thousand yards I was able to see the enemy force for the first time. With my head stuck out of the director hatch, I could discern a battleship on our port side. By the time [Rangefinder Operator J.W.] Shelton said, "Range three thousand yards," I recognized the gigantic superstructure of a *Kongō*-class battleship. She looked like the Empire State Building to me. We had chosen this ship (the *Hiei*) as our target right from the start and had a perfect solution on her.

—C. RAYMOND CALHOUN, *TIN CAN SAILOR: LIFE ABOARD THE USS* STERETT, *1939–1945*

OPEN FIRE!

On board the *Atlanta*, Captain Jenkins called for counter-illumination. His gunnery officer, Lieutenant Commander W. R. D. Nickelson, was more assertive: "Counter-illuminate, hell! Fire!" The *Atlanta*'s guns started shooting at the *Hiei*'s searchlights from a range of just 1,600 yards. As his ship fired rapidly at the Japanese battleship, Jenkins and his bridge crew sighted other targets in the darkness. With two main battery directors and 16 5-inch guns, the *Atlanta* was well-suited to confused, close-range brawls. Jenkins kept the aft battery focused on the *Hiei* and diverted the forward group to a destroyer.

> Two enemy destroyers were sighted crossing the line of fire from left to right, on course about North. They were clearly identified in the searchlight beam as Japanese destroyers similar to the *Asashio* class. . . . Fire of the forward group . . . was shifted from the illuminating vessel to the rear destroyer, which was seen to receive about twenty hits in the hull from 1200 yards range, erupt in flame, and later disappear.

—CAPTAIN SAMUEL P. JENKINS, COMMANDING OFFICER, USS *ATLANTA*, 20 NOVEMBER 1942

The *Atlanta*'s forward guns fired on the *Akatsuki*. Her searchlight made her a visible target, and many of Callaghan's ships, including the *Laffey*, *O'Bannon*, *Atlanta*, *San Francisco*, *Helena*, *Aaron Ward*, and *Fletcher*, fired at Captain Yusuke Yamada's Destroyer Division 6 flagship.

Lieutenant (junior grade) Edward D. Corboy controlled the *Atlanta*'s aft battery. He spotted the opening salvo as short 400 yards and quickly corrected, and 5-inch shells began to tear into the *Hiei*'s superstructure. With the *Atlanta* trapped in the searchlight beams and illuminated by her own rapid gunfire, several Japanese ships began to concentrate on her. Captain Masao Nishida directed *Hiei*'s 14-inch guns to fire on the light cruiser. Bombardment shells exploded against the superstructure, wrecking the forward gun mounts. The *Nagara*, *Inazuma*, and *Ikazuchi* also aimed their guns at the "Lucky A." Shells burst within the light cruiser's hull and superstructure, as ammunition in the forward mounts and nearby antiaircraft guns began to explode.

A dramatic photograph of cruiser *Atlanta*, coming alongside the *San Francisco* to refuel on 16 October 1942. While serving as Rear Admiral Norman Scott's flagship the night of 12–13 November, the *Atlanta* was seriously damaged by Japanese and U.S. fire. Her captain, Captain Samuel P. Jenkins, scuttled her the next morning. (Naval History and Heritage Command)

At that time two heavy jolts were felt, the first possibly a torpedo hit forward, and the second definitely a torpedo hit in the forward engine room. Both of these were distinctly heavier and different in character from our gunfire hits. All power except auxiliary diesel was lost, our fire was interrupted, and steering control has to be shifted to the steering engine room. At about the same time all . . . gunfire against *Atlanta* ceased, and illumination went out. The illuminating ship, which had been under fire also by another ship of our force, was seen to sink.

—CAPTAIN SAMUEL P. JENKINS, COMMANDING OFFICER, USS *ATLANTA*, 20 NOVEMBER 1942

The *Inazuma* and *Ikazuchi*, trailing behind the *Akatsuki*, each launched six torpedoes at the U.S. line from about 1,000 yards. One of these found the *Atlanta*, knocking out her power and her guns and causing a 10-degree list to port.

From the head of the column, the *Cushing* opened fire on a Japanese destroyer—possibly the *Amatsukaze* or *Yukikaze*—which was rapidly approaching on the starboard bow and about 2,000 yards away. The *Cushing's* captain, Lieutenant Commander Edward N. Parker, thought he was hitting effectively, but the Japanese destroyer remained undamaged. The *Laffey* had been tracking targets to starboard but quickly shifted to port and opened fire on the *Akatsuki*. Lieutenant Charles R. Calhoun thought the *Sterret* hit an enemy ship with her second salvo. The Japanese also found the range. Hits on the *Sterret's* port side wrecked the steering gear and ignited ammunition, illuminating the destroyer. The destroyer drifted out of line. Her mast was hit, knocking out radars, emergency identification lights, and the TBS antenna. Shrapnel flew through the director, injuring Calhoun's crew. On board the *O'Bannon*, Commander Edwin R. Wilkinson tried to keep his ship from colliding with the careening *Sterett*. He had to go "hard right" and then "hard left" before settling on course 270. During these maneuvers, Wilkinson opened fire on the searchlights on the port bow and sent more shells toward the *Akatsuki*.

Astern of the *Atlanta*, the *San Francisco* came around to port. Her gunners also focused on the *Akatsuki*, which they misidentified as a cruiser, a common mistake that night. The flames from the crippled destroyer appeared to reach "a thousand feet into the air."

The *San Francisco* fired first at an enemy cruiser on starboard hand and that ship was hit heavily with about seven main battery salvoes. This target was taken under fire by other of our ships and is believed to have been destroyed. Control was ordered to shift targets by Captain and fire was opened on a small cruiser or large destroyer further ahead on starboard bow. She was hit with two full main battery salvoes and set afire throughout her length.

—LIEUTENANT COMMANDER H. E. SCHONLAND, USS *SAN FRANCISCO*, 16 NOVEMBER 1942

The *San Francisco's* second target was the *Atlanta* and, unfortunately, the shooting was incredibly accurate; roughly 19 hits were scored from just three or four salvoes. One of them put seven shells into the forward superstructure. Although they did not explode, the shells tore through the flag plot, pilot house, and radio room, killing Admiral Scott and all but one of his staff. Captain Jenkins was thrown against a watertight door. The navigator, Lieutenant Commander J. S. Smith Jr., urged Jenkins to move to the secondary conning station. Although mortally wounded, Smith remained on the bridge and tried to fight the ship while Jenkins

Damage to the *Akatsuki*

[Lieutenant Michiharu] Shinya was knocked flat. Blood trickled into his right eye from a head wound, and a piece of shrapnel was embedded in his right cheek. He heard Captain Yamada order port helm (why did Commander [Osamu] Takasuka not give the order?), but the helmsman was dead. Shinya reached out to turn the wheel. When the wheel did not respond, he called out, "She's not answering the helm!" and then struggled to his feet. His hat and shoes had been blown off. The deck was slippery—with blood—and his head was ringing. He heard Takasuka calling to the gunnery officer, but there was no response.

The bridge reeked of high explosive. Shinya's eyes picked out the living—Captain Yamada, Commander Takasuka, the navigator, and his assistant—and the dead, the division's medical officer and paymaster, the helmsman, talkers, lookouts, and Shinya's torpedo director crew. If Shinya and his assistant had not changed places, and if the shell(s) had not hit the rear of the bridge, he would have been among the dead.

—JAMES W. GRACE, *THE NAVAL BATTLE OF GUADALCANAL*

An impressive view of the destroyer *O'Bannon*, fourth ship in Callaghan's line, probably taken in 1943. She was the only one of Callaghan's van destroyers equipped with an SG radar, visible near the top of her mast, below the SC antenna. (National Archives)

responsible. After it "exploded," Shanklin checked fire and found a new target.

Visibility at this point was poor, as flares were burning between the two forces and the smoke from gunfire was getting heavy. This second target was not positively identified, but is believed to have been either a light or heavy cruiser. Two nine-gun salvoes were fired, and several hits from each salvo were observed. The after FC radar was functioning perfectly and the opening range was right on.

—LIEUTENANT COMMANDER E. W. SHANKLIN, GUNNERY OFFICER, USS *PORTLAND*, 14 NOVEMBER 1942

The *Portland*'s second target was probably the *Ikazuchi*. She was damaged by a series of 8-inch hits from U.S. cruisers, which knocked out two of her turrets and set fire to the forward handling room. As ammunition started to explode below the forecastle, her captain, Commander Saneo Maeda, considered abandoning ship.

Captain Hoover's *Helena* followed the *Portland*. As at Cape Esperance, the *Helena* was probably the first ship on either side to open fire. Lieutenant Commander Rodman Smith, the gunnery officer, had his gun directors and radars tracking targets well before visual contact was made. When the searchlights snapped on, Smith was ready: "Commence firing was ordered immediately and the main battery opened fire in continuous fire at a range of about 4200 yards." Her spotters noted that "our tracers appeared to be perfect in deflection and that practically all of our shots appeared to hit." Like many other ships, the *Helena* put her initial salvoes into the *Akatsuki*.

Next in the column, the *Juneau* had been briefly illuminated by a powerful Japanese searchlight before it settled on the *Helena*. Lieutenant Commander Warren Graf, the *Juneau*'s gunnery officer, initially aimed at the largest available target, Abe's flagship *Hiei*. However,

moved aft. Callaghan recognized the error and ordered over TBS, "Cease firing own ships."

In the meantime, the *Portland* had joined the fight. She had been tracking enemy ships with her SG radar since about 0142 and had coached her FC radar onto a target. As she followed the *San Francisco* around to port, the gun turrets and director swung to maintain bearing. Captain Laurance T. DuBose ordered Lieutenant Commander E. W. Shanklin, the gunnery officer, to open fire: "When the first salvo landed at least four bursts of flame leapt from the enemy vessel, which by this time was recognized as a destroyer. The second salvo was fired, and the destroyer exploded and sank immediately." Shanklin was probably also firing at the *Akatsuki*. So many ships were hitting the hapless destroyer that it was difficult to know who was doing the damage, but DuBose thought the *Portland* was he quickly shifted to a more imminent threat, the destroyer *Yūdachi*. Commander Kiyoshi Kikkawa's destroyer had passed ahead of the U.S. formation before the shooting started, reversed course, and was now rapidly approaching from starboard. She fired a salvo of torpedoes at the American cruisers and then opened fire with her guns. Kikkawa thought the range was too close for an effective turn away; he resolved to pass through the enemy line, in the gap between the *Juneau* and the *Aaron Ward*. Captain Lyman K. Swenson of the *Juneau* had ordered his automatic weapons crews to hold their fire, afraid the flashes from their guns would reveal the location of his ship, but as the *Yudachi* closed and her shells passed through masts and rigging overhead, the automatic weapons opened fire. A stream of tracers reached out toward the approaching destroyer.

"THE FOURTH OF JULY IN HELL"

Astern of the *Juneau*, Captain Tobin tried to maintain the cohesion of his four-destroyer group from the bridge of the *Aaron Ward*. When the searchlights reached out, his ships immediately opened fire.

The *Ikazuchi* Is Hit

In *Ikazuchi*'s gunnery telephone control room, Petty Officer Hashimoto was suddenly thrown out of his chair and into the fuze panel. After several more jolts, the lights went out and the communication went dead. There had been hits behind the bridge, at the base of the superstructure, and on mount one. As smoke drifted in, the flames provided illumination. The crew immediately began searching for the gas masks that they should have been carrying. Hashimoto was closest to the shelf where they had been left and passed them out to the other four men.

The lights came back on, but there was still no contact with other sections of the ship. A couple of men were sent to check on the gun mounts while another man continued to call them through the voice pipe. A man named Kokubu called down from the gun director, claiming that he was all alone, and asked permission to come below. Assuming that everyone else was dead, Petty Officer Mitsumiya granted the request.

—JAMES W. GRACE, *THE NAVAL BATTLE OF GUADALCANAL* (NAVAL INSTITUTE PRESS, 1999)

At about 0149 an enemy ship on port beam of our column illuminated our cruisers by searchlights. Our forces opened fire on the enemy. Ships of this group [the rear destroyers] took ships on port bow under fire. At about 0152, *Barton* fired five torpedoes to port, but there is no information relative to hits. At 0153, *Monssen* fired five torpedoes to starboard. . . . Two torpedo hits on target between forward super-structure and mainmast were observed.

—CAPTAIN ROBERT G. TOBIN, COMMANDER, DESTROYER SQUADRON 12, USS *AARON WARD*, 27 NOVEMBER 1942

Callaghan ordered Tobin's destroyers to take course 000 and steam through the Japanese formation in the wake of Stokes's van group. Tobin tried to maintain that course as the battle raged around his ships. Tobin's flagship, the *Aaron Ward*, had been tracking a large target since 0145. When the searchlights flashed on, her captain, Commander Orville F. Gregor opened fire on the *Hiei* from 7,000 yards. Ten salvoes were fired before one of Callaghan's cruisers fouled the range. Gregor "observed many small fires and explosions" but was uncertain if his guns were responsible. The *Hiei* returned fire, hitting the *Aaron Ward* with at least three shells that damaged the forward part of the ship, cutting communication cables and starting a fire.

As the *Yūdachi* closed the U.S. line, the *Harusame* followed behind her. She appeared out of the darkness on the *Aaron Ward*'s starboard bow. The two destroyers were just 1,200 yards apart and on a collision course. Gregor stopped the engines and then backed them. Crewmen amidships watched two torpedo wakes approach from port; they appeared to pass directly under the ship. A high-pitched whine passed through the hull as the "fish" passed by, sending a chill through those below decks.

As the *Aaron Ward* slowed, the *Barton* moved up on her starboard side. Lieutenant Commander Douglas H. Fox's destroyer was firing rapidly at a target to port when she was hit in quick succession by two torpedoes. The *Barton* disappeared in a brilliant explosion. There was no time to abandon ship. Only 42 men survived, and just two escaped from the ship's interior. After the *Barton* vanished, darkness closed in again. Lieutenant Commander Charles E. McCombs of the *Monssen* sighted the *Hiei* about 4,000 yards off the starboard bow. McCombs had told his torpedo officer, Ensign Robert Lasseen, to fire on his own initiative

when a satisfactory target was located. Lasseen fired five torpedoes immediately. All seem to have missed, perhaps because Lasseen and McCombs thought the Japanese flagship was dead in the water.

At the rear of the column, Commander William Cole and his executive officer, Lieutenant Commander Joseph Wylie, had an excellent picture of the developing battle from on board the *Fletcher*. The two of them had worked out an effective arrangement to fight the ship at night. Wylie stood at the edge of the radar room, where he could observe the SG display, track potential targets, and monitor the column's movement. He gave a clear sense of the battle to Cole and the ship's gun and torpedo batteries. The *Fletcher*'s guns opened fire, probably at the *Akatsuki*, when the searchlights came on and then quickly shifted to a new target, one Cole identified as a cruiser. It may have been the *Nagara*, hit once during the opening stage of the battle.

THE *SAN FRANCISCO* ALONE

Callaghan initially ordered a cease-fire because the *San Francisco* was firing on the *Atlanta*, but he repeated it for the rest of his cruisers. This controversial order seemingly makes no sense. Why, in the middle of a tense firefight, would the admiral order a cease-fire? Callaghan was putting his desperate plan in motion. He recognized that his cruisers had a clear path to the center of the Japanese formation; Tobin's destroyers had broken through the enemy screen. Callaghan's next task was to locate the enemy battleships and then close to decisive range with his cruisers. He expected a brief pause—like those undertaken by various ships at Cape Esperance to reorient themselves—would allow him to accomplish both these things.

The *Barton* Explodes

Without further notification and at approximately 0145 the leading ships of our column were observed to commence firing to port. Several batteries of searchlights on apparently large enemy ships were trained on our unit from that side. The *Barton* immediately opened fire with the forward two 5-in guns to port, and continued firing rapidly, expending approximately sixty rounds. The after battery opened fire to port a few seconds later and fired approximately ten rounds per gun; then became silent and could not be brought to bear on enemy ships. The *Barton* was observed to change course to port, moving closer to the enemy column, and was seen to launch one torpedo in the general direction of the leading enemy ship, followed a few seconds later by the other four. It was not observed . . . whether hits were scored on the target or not. After about seven minutes of continued firing the *Barton* had stopped to avoid collision with an unidentified friendly ship ahead when one torpedo, evidently from enemy column to the right, struck the forward fire room on the starboard side. A few seconds later a second torpedo struck the forward engine room and the ship broke in two and sank in approximately ten seconds. Survivors from the *Barton* are few and the total number is not known at this time.

—LIEUTENANT (JUNIOR GRADE) HARLOWE M. WHITE, SENIOR SURVIVING OFFICER, USS *BARTON*, 26 NOVEMBER 1942

Callaghan's orders make this clear. Upon receiving the command to cease fire, Captain DuBose immediately asked for clarification: "Want me to cease firing?" He followed with the more informal query, "What is the dope?" The admiral repeated the order to cease firing and ordered a course change to the north. He aimed to cross behind the stern of Abe's flagship and

The battleship *Hiei*, pictured in the 1930s, while she was serving as a training ship. Under the terms of the London Treaty of 1930, she was demilitarized. Her aftmost turret was removed along with her belt armor. Before the war, she was rebuilt and used as a testbed for the sophisticated fire control systems of the large battleships *Yamato* and *Musashi*. The *Hiei* was the flagship of Rear Admiral Hiroaki Abe during the Guadalcanal Campaign; she was lost after a close-range melee with U.S. Navy ships at the First Naval Battle of Guadalcanal. (Naval History and Heritage Command)

announced to his cruisers: "Battleship on starboard bow. Destroyers all around and cruisers. . . . take place in column astern." As the range closed, he ordered the *San Francisco* to open fire. The *Hiei* was so close that the cruiser's guns, which loaded at 9 degrees elevation, had to *depress* to come onto the target.

As the *San Francisco* dueled with the *Hiei*, Callaghan tried to coordinate the firepower of his cruisers. He hoped the *Portland* and *Helena* would come into action behind him, but even though *Portland* was close astern, Captain DuBose could not identify the *Hiei*. He repeatedly asked for her bearing. In the meantime, the *Portland* had begun firing at a cruiser, 7,000 yards away on the starboard beam. This was probably the destroyer *Ikazuchi*, then engaged with the *Atlanta*. After the *Portland* fired her second salvo at this target, a torpedo from the destroyer *Yūdachi* hit her stern, shattering the aft deck and bending hull plating into a massive rudder. The ship turned in circles to starboard, unable to straighten its course. DuBose recounted: "As the first swing to the right was completed a *Haruna* type battleship became clearly visible. Fire was opened on the battleship and continued by the forward turrets throughout the swing, four hitting salvoes being fired, range 4000 yards."

Once the *Portland* started firing at the *Hiei*, DuBose no longer needed precise bearings. Callaghan told him, "Give her hell." But DuBose would never receive the message; the *Portland*'s TBS had been knocked out by the shock of the torpedo hit. She would only fire

those four salvoes. As she continued to steam in circles, the action moved beyond her. Callaghan later asked DuBose if he had the battleship, but never received a response. The admiral and his crew continued to fight the *Hiei* alone.

Three searchlights shot out from the battleship to help her gunners find the range. They fixed on the *San Francisco*, illuminating the cruiser. On their third salvo, the *Hiei*'s gunners scored. A 14-inch bombardment shell slammed into the *San Francisco*'s pilothouse, killing or wounding most of the men on the bridge. Captain Young fell unconscious. The battle had reached its decisive moment. Although Callaghan had failed to bring his three large cruisers into action simultaneously, his flagship was pouring a heavy fire into the *Hiei* at point-blank range. Surviving officers estimated that the *San Francisco* hit the battleship at least 18 times. Fires broke out on board the *Hiei*, and her main guns stopped firing. But Callaghan's moment of triumph was brief; the *Kirishima*, hidden in the darkness to port, opened fire. From starboard, Commander Hara's *Amatsukaze* approached at high speed, firing as she closed the range. Another Japanese ship—the cruiser *Nagara*—also opened fire on Callaghan's flagship.

San Francisco engaged enemy battleship on starboard bow. This ship used a group of three searchlights in a triangular arrangement, two over one. Simultaneously, we were being fired upon by a cruiser on our starboard quarter who was also il-

The cruiser *Portland*, photographed at Pearl Harbor on 14 June 1942. Note the overall gray color scheme and the FC radar antenna atop her main battery director. The *Portland* followed Callaghan's flagship the night of 12–13 November until her stern was destroyed by a Japanese torpedo. She cruised in circles the rest of the night and sank the destroyer *Yūdachi* with well-placed 8-inch salvoes that morning. (Naval History and Heritage Command)

The battleship *Hiei* as she appeared in 1941. She has been rebuilt after her time as a training ship and is ready for war. Note the large director and rangefinder atop her foremast, the row of 6-inch guns amidships, and the many searchlights around her forward stack. (Wenger Collection via Mr. Masataka Chihaya)

The battleship *Kirishima* is pictured between the world wars. She was modernized before the start of World War II. During November 1942, she was twice sent to bombard Henderson Field and was twice thwarted by Navy task forces. (U.S. Naval Institute Photo Archive)

luminating us. An enemy destroyer cut across our starboard bow, came down our port side on reverse course firing at us with all of his battery. *San Francisco* was now being hit heavily from three directions. The battleship started hitting on his third salvo, the cruiser on about his second salvo. The 5-in port battery engaged the destroyer on the port hand but was out of action almost immediately except for gun Number 8, which continued firing in local control, and hit the destroyer in the vicinity of his depth charge racks.

—LIEUTENANT COMMANDER H. E. SCHONLAND, USS *SAN FRANCISCO*, 16 NOVEMBER 1942

With the *San Francisco* fighting four Japanese ships singlehandedly, Captain Hoover of the *Helena* asked permission to open fire. Callaghan wanted to make sure she was focused on the enemy battleships, responding, "want to get the big ones." Hoover did not respond but felt confident in his targets.

The identity of *Helena*'s target is uncertain. Her main battery apparently focused on the *Hiei*, pouring out a murderous fire. According to Bureau of Ordnance records, each of the cruiser's 6-inch guns could fire at a rate of ten rounds per minute, but in practice, the *Helena* and her crew had fired 17 rounds per minute. "Fifteen streams of liquid fire" converged on the Japanese flagship; Callaghan's plan was working. Smith directed the *Helena*'s secondary guns onto the *Amatsukaze*, starting fires, wrecking the destroyer's hydraulic system, and disabling her control systems. The crew of the *San Francisco* received some respite, but the cruiser was in desperate shape.

Japanese shells slammed into the *San Francisco*'s hull and superstructure. Callaghan and most of his staff were cut down by a 6-inch shell from the *Hiei*'s secondary battery. Lieutenant Commander Herbert E. Schonland quickly became the *San Francisco*'s senior surviving officer. From his position in central station

The extent of the *San Francisco*'s damage is plain in this photograph, taken on 14 December 1942 at the Mare Island Navy Yard. Each white circle is a shell hit. (National Archives)

At about 0203, radar plot reported at least six enemy ships on our starboard hand heading in a northerly direction. While putting the main battery on one of these targets, one was observed to be firing on the *San Francisco* then on our starboard bow. Both FC radars got on this target and at 0204 opened fire with the main battery in full automatic using forward FC radar in train. Opening range was 8800 yards. Fired for approximately 1½ to 2 minutes and ceased firing at range of 9400 yards when *San Francisco* on our starboard hand came in line of fire.

—CAPTAIN GILBERT C. HOOVER, COMMANDING OFFICER, USS *HELENA*, 15 NOVEMBER 1942

below decks, he focused on damage control. As shell hits knocked out control stations, he shifted the conn. When the bridge was disabled, he shifted it to the aft battle station. The acting executive officer, Commander Joe Hubbard, took over, but a 14-inch shell from the *Kirishima* slammed into Hubbard's position, killing him and his men. Schonland shifted control again, this time to the armored conning tower, where Quartermaster Third Class Floyd A. Rogers took the helm. Lieutenant Commander Bruce McCandless, the only officer on the bridge still standing, joined Rogers and informed Schonland that he was the senior surviving officer.

The destroyer *Amatsukaze*. Commander Tameichi Hara captained her during the First Naval Battle of Guadalcanal. The *Amatsukaze* was disabled by gunfire from the cruiser *Helena*, but Hara was able to withdraw from the battle. (U.S. Naval Institute Photo Archive)

Boatswain's Mate First Class Reinhard J. Keppler. Keppler singlehandedly fought fires in the *San Francisco*'s hangar the night of 12–13 November and was mortally wounded by shrapnel. Once others joined him, he directed their efforts until he collapsed. Keppler was posthumously awarded the Medal of Honor for his part in saving the ship. (Naval History and Heritage Command)

The *Helena* Fires on the *Amatsukaze*

My head snapped to that direction, and there was another enemy cruiser. I stood frozen from head to toe, but finally yelled, "Douse searchlight, stop shelling, spread smoke screen!" I had not finished the order when the third salvo from the new enemy, later identified as *Helena*, reached *Amatsukaze*. Two shells landed very near. I hunched my back and clung to the railing. The blast was so strong, it almost threw me off the bridge. The detonations were deafening. I got sluggishly to my feet, but my mind was a complete blank for several seconds. Next, I felt over my body, but found no wounds.

Looking around I saw with relief that all my nearby fellow officers were alive. What about others? I saw Iwata prostrate, hanging over the range-finding gear. "Iwata, Iwata," I cried. "What's the matter with you?" He did not move. Blood covered his head. A piece of shrapnel had pierced his skull, killing him instantly.

—CAPTAIN TAMEICHI HARA, *JAPANESE DESTROYER CAPTAIN* (NAVAL INSTITUTE PRESS, 1967, 2011)

So that he could continue to oversee damage control efforts, Schonland delegated command of the ship to McCandless. Farther aft, a dangerous fire raged in the hanger amidships. Boatswain's Mate First Class Reinhard J. Keppler fought it alone as shells exploded around him. His calm determination inspired others to join the effort; Keppler directed the firefighting and assisted wounded men before collapsing to the deck, overcome by loss of blood.

GENERAL MELEE

While Admiral Callaghan was bringing his flagship to decisive range, the destroyer *Cushing* was slicing through the Japanese formation. She had been firing at an enemy destroyer when the Japanese flagship appeared close at hand, bearing down from the port side. The *Hiei*'s secondary and antiaircraft batteries opened fire. At the same time, two other ships—a destroyer on the port side and an unidentified ship to starboard—

Excerpt from the *San Francisco's* TBS Log

Time	Recipients	Message
0146	From CTF 67.4	Enemy on starboard and ---- bow also same on port bow. Stand by to open fire.
	Atlanta from CTF 67.4	What are you doing?
	CTF 67.4 from *Atlanta*	Avoiding own destroyers crossing.
	Van Destroyers from CTF 67.4	Come back to original course.
	From Van Destroyers	Roger
	CTF 67.4 from *Helena*	Have several targets on port bow.
0147	Van Destroyers from CTF 67.4	What do you have on starboard now?
	Van Destroyers from CTF 67.4	Are you back on course?
	CTF 67.4 from *Juneau*	Have ------
	From CTF 67.4	All ships commence firing to starboard. [Note this was recorded incorrectly on board the *San Francisco*]
0149	From CTF 67.4	All ships hold your course now.
0151	From CTF 67.4	Cease firing, our ships.
	CTF 67.4 from *Portland*	Want me to cease firing?
	CTF 67.4 from *Portland*	What is the dope?
0154	*Portland* from CTF 67.4	Cease firing all ships take ------
	CTF 67.4 from *Portland*	Authenticate that please.
	TF 67.4 from CTF 67.4	All ships take course 000°.
	CTF 67.4 from *Barton* (?)	Where is enemy?
	From CTF 67.4	Battleship on starboard bow. Destroyers all around and cruisers. All ships take place in column astern.
0155	CTF 67.4	True bearing of battleship? This is Portland.
	CTF 67.4 from *Portland*	True bearing is what?
	From CTF 67.4	Portland is ---ing.
	Portland from CTF 67.4	Give her hell.
0156	*Portland* from CTF 67.4	Acknowledge.
	Van Destroyers from *Laffey*	Testing.
0156	*Laffey* from Van Destroyers	Receiving you OK.
0157	CTF 67.4 from *Helena*	Four ships in column 060.
	From *Sterett*	Have a jammed rudder, is alright now would -----
	From *Laffey* (?)	Turn on lights for about three seconds.
0200	*Portland* from CTF 67.4	Do you have battleship, if so open fire.
	CTF 67.4 from *Helena*	Request permission to open fire if we have targets
	Helena from CTF 67.4	Advise type of targets first want to get the big ones.
	Portland from CTF 67.4	Do you have battleship?
	Portland from CTF 67.4	We think we have.
	Portland from CTF 67.4	-----------

DASHED LINES INDICATE AREAS WHERE THE WORDING IS MISSING OR ILLEGIBLE BECAUSE OF BATTLE DAMAGE.

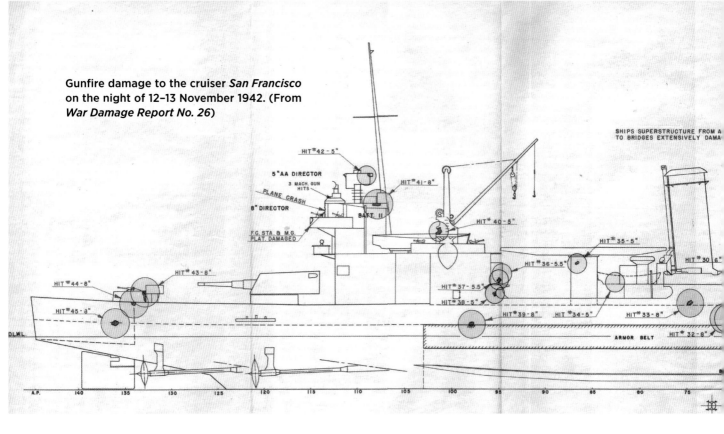

Gunfire damage to the cruiser *San Francisco* on the night of 12–13 November 1942. (From *War Damage Report No. 26*)

were firing at the *Cushing*. All four 5-inch mounts were hit. The gun director was disabled. Shrapnel tore through steam lines in the forward fire room; a hit in the aft fire room cut the flow of feed water to the boiler, and it burned up. All power was lost; lubrication ceased flowing to the main engines and their bearings burnt out. The *Cushing* was adrift.

The *Laffey* was next in line. Lieutenant (junior grade) Tom Evins was manning the torpedo director and looking for a good target when the *Hiei*'s towering superstructure appeared out of the gloom less than 1,000 yards away. As the battleship closed, Evins trained his battery around and fired a salvo of five torpedoes. Captain Nishida took evasive action; he avoided the first one. Two others slammed into the battleship's hull and failed to explode. The range was too close for them to arm. The *Hiei* kept coming. Lieutenant William K. Ratliff, the gunnery officer, watched the battleship from his position in the main battery director. He opened fire at 200 yards, and 5-inch shells slammed into the battleship's superstructure. The *Laffey*'s captain, Lieutenant Commander William E. Hank, accelerated and put the helm over to avoid a collision. The stern fishtailed as the destroyer turned to port, carving a path around the *Hiei*'s bow. The ships passed within ten yards of each other as automatic weapons on both ships opened fire.

Since the *Sterett* had sheered out of line, the *O'Bannon* came next. Commander Wilkinson used Callaghan's "cease fire" order to momentarily check fire and reorient himself. He had lost contact with the *Cushing* and *Laffey* and appeared to be at the head of

Aboard the *Hiei*

On the starboard wing of *Hiei*'s bridge, Lieutenant Commander Chihaya of the admiral's staff had his binoculars on the *Laffey*, bemoaning the absence of rams on modern ships, so close was the range when the destroyer opened fire. The *Hiei*'s superstructure was raked by 5-in, 1.1-in, and 20-mm gunfire. Bursting shells illuminated her bridge interior to the destroyer's crew. Three hits from the port side crashed into *Hiei*'s bridge, breaking glass, scattering fragments, and cutting down men left and right. Cdr. Masakane Suzuki, the chief of staff, was killed instantly and fell against Chihaya, just behind him. Then shrapnel tore through Chihaya's hands. Admiral Abe was hit in the face, and as Captain Nishida called for a corpsman and went to his aid, the captain was knocked to the deck with a badly slashed calf. Nishida refused to go below with the corpsman; instead he bandaged himself with a seaman's neckerchief.

—JAMES W. GRACE, *THE NAVAL BATTLE OF GUADALCANAL* (NAVAL INSTITUTE PRESS, 1999)

UNITED STATES NAVAL INSTITUTE

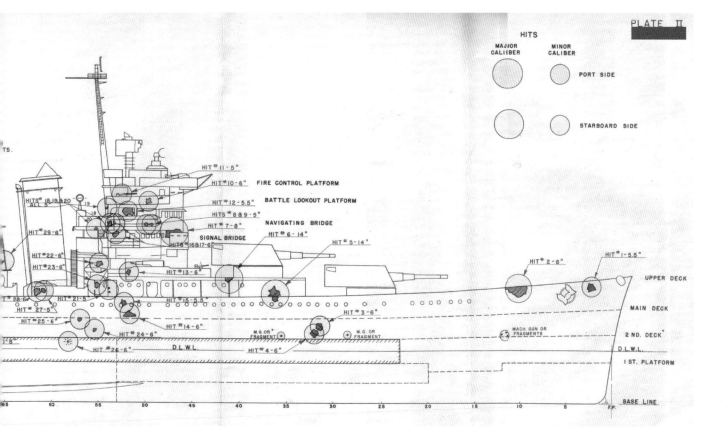

PLATE II

HITS

MAJOR CALIBER | MINOR CALIBER

PORT SIDE

STARBOARD SIDE

HIT # 11 - 5"
HIT # 10 - 6" FIRE CONTROL PLATFORM
HIT # 12 - 5.5" BATTLE LOOKOUT PLATFORM
HITS # 8 & 9 - 5"
HIT # 7 - 8" NAVIGATING BRIDGE
HIT # 6 - 14"
HIT # 5 - 14'
HITS # 18,19,&20 ALL 5"
HIT # 29 - 6"
SIGNAL BRIDGE
HIT 6-16&17-6"
HIT # 2 - 8"
HIT # 1 - 5.5"
UPPER DECK
HIT # 22 - 6"
HIT # 23 - 6"
HIT # 13 - 6"
MAIN DECK
HIT # 21 - 5"
HIT # 15 - 5.5"
HIT # 28 - 6"
HIT # 27 - 5"
HIT # 3 - 6"
2 ND. DECK
MACH. GUN OR FRAGMENTS
HIT # 25 - 6"
HIT # 24 - 6"
M.G. OR FRAGMENT
M.G. OR FRAGMENT
D.L.W.L.
HIT # 26 - 6"
D.L.W.L.
HIT # 14 - 6"
HIT # 4 - 6"
I ST. PLATFORM
BASE LINE

the column. Wilkinson sighted an enemy cruiser 3,000 yards away on the starboard side and opened fire. Then he saw Abe's flagship approaching from the opposite side. He ordered, "Torpedo action to port!" The range was less than 1,200 yards. As the *O'Bannon* approached the battleship, Wilkinson put on full power astern and went hard right to avoid a collision.

Although damaged, the *Sterett* was still able to fight. Commander Jesse Coward had compensated for the loss of her steering gear by steering with the engines. He followed the other van destroyers as best he could and was soon passing close to the *Hiei*. Lieutenant Calhoun opened fire from just 2,000 yards. Although damaged, the *Hiei* was able to return fire. She hit the

The *Sterett,* the third destroyer in Callaghan's column, photographed on 26 May 1942. Commander Jesse Coward conned his ship successfully through the melee and was able to escort Callaghan's surviving cruisers back to Nouméa. (National Archives)

Sterett with three 14-inch shells. One started a fire in the handling room for Mount 3; another wiped out the gun crew. Coward wisely withdrew from the close-range encounter. Despite the serious damage to his ship, he and his officers continued to look for potential targets.

Herbert E. Schonland (left) and Bruce McCandless, pictured as commanders in December 1942, after bringing the *San Francisco* back to the United States. They led the efforts to save the cruiser and extricate her from the battle after Rear Admiral Callaghan was killed and Captain Young was mortally wounded. For their actions, they were each awarded the Medal of Honor. (Naval History and Heritage Command)

Conditions on board the *Hiei* were worse. After close encounters with Callaghan's van destroyers, dueling with the *San Francisco*, and receiving fire from the other cruisers, the Japanese battleship had lost central control of her main battery. Turrets were operating in local control, significantly reducing their accuracy. At least 25 large-caliber shells had penetrated the superstructure; many others had hit the hull. The *Cushing*, *Laffey*, *Sterett*, and *San Francisco* had raked the *Hiei*'s bridge with automatic weapons fire. Communications had been knocked out, isolating Abe from the rest of his formation. He abandoned his bombardment mission and focused on extricating his ships from Ironbottom Sound.

Admiral Callaghan's line had disintegrated. The *Atlanta* was crippled, the *Portland* was out of control, the *Barton* had exploded, and the *San Francisco* was struggling to survive. As ships lost contact with each other, they fought individual battles in the darkness. Schonland noted, "The action developed into a melee and targets were fired upon as opportunity offered them." Tobin's assessment was similar: "After the battle started it was pretty much a matter of every ship for itself."

The *Sterett* Engages the *Hiei*

She had absorbed all that our cruisers could dish out and was on fire from her bridge aft. She was making very little headway; I estimated her speed to be under five knots as she steamed in front of us. She was a perfect target. Beautifully illuminated by her own fires, her superstructure towered high above us, and I instructed Byers to train his sights on her "pagoda," or bridge structure. Before he had even trained around that far, the word came from the bridge to open fire. The instant that Byers reported, "On target," I repeated the commence fire order to the gun and director crews. We poured nine salvoes (thirty-six projectiles) into that bridge structure, and I could see them explode against it. At that range, every shot hit its mark, and those thirty-six 5-in shells raised plenty of hell over there with any officers or men who were exposed. By this time we were less than 1000 yards away, and we could see several Japanese sailors dive overboard with their

clothes on fire. I told the gun crews what their work had accomplished, and over my telephone I could hear them cheer as the news was relayed to them by their captains.

Tom McWhorter fired a full salvo of four torpedoes at the target. I saw two red explosions in the water a couple of minutes after hearing the "fish" leave their tubes; other *Sterett* observers also reported seeing them. It appeared that we had scored two hits in the engineering spaces (although subsequent assessments did not give the *Sterett* credit for them). The fires topside seemed to flare up, and once more I saw crew members running along her main deck and jumping overboard. She was dead in the water and burning fiercely when we left her. We crossed her bow no more than 500 yards ahead of her—so close that she could not lower her guns far enough to hit us.

—C. RAYMOND CALHOUN, *TIN CAN SAILOR: LIFE ABOARD THE USS* STERETT, *1939–1945* (NAVAL INSTITUTE PRESS, 2000)

Tobin had a clear view of the breakdown of the U.S. formation. As the Japanese destroyers *Yūdachi* and *Harusame* passed through the column ahead of his flagship, the *Aaron Ward*, the *Juneau* hit the *Yūdachi* on the bridge, killing one man and wounding several more. The *Aaron Ward* also hit Commander Kikkawa's ship. Kikkawa laid a smokescreen to cover his escape. The *Harusame* followed but lost the *Yūdachi* in a "forest of shell splashes." On board the *Aaron Ward*, Commander Gregor accelerated away from the confusion and brought his ship back to course 000. He and his crew sighted the *Hiei* 1,500 yards away on the port side and prepared to fire torpedoes, but the *San Francisco* got in the way. Then a destroyer appeared out of the darkness. She was the *Sterett*. Commander Coward almost opened fire, but he recognized the friendly profile of the *Aaron Ward* in time.

At about 0206, Gregor sighted another target showing "fighting lights of a single cluster, white over red over green." This was not a U.S. arrangement, so he opened fire. Gregor identified the target as a "cruiser of the *Katori* class." It might have been the *Nagara*. After he lost it, Gregor shifted to a new target, a searchlight off the port bow. He changed course to starboard to open the *Aaron Ward*'s broadside and opened fire: "Four salvoes were fired from the director control, which was then hit. Guns continued to fire in local control by manual, firing approximately seven salvoes." Gregor's target was probably the *Yūdachi*. The two ships exchanged fire, and the *Aaron Ward* was damaged. The director was knocked out, the topmast was shot away, and the forward engine room lost power.

Another ship opened fire on her, hitting the aft part of the ship, starting fires, destroying antiaircraft guns, and igniting depth charges. These shells were probably fired by the *San Francisco*, which had misidentified Tobin's flagship and was desperately trying to survive. After a searchlight illuminated the *Aaron Ward*, Gregor

The destroyer *Monssen* passes mail to the carrier *Enterprise* in the South Pacific on 19 May 1942. The *Monssen* was one of Callaghan's rear destroyers. She was crippled during the battle and eventually abandoned. Her hulk blew up and sank about noon the following day. (Naval History and Heritage Command)

divided his fire—even guns to starboard and odd to port—to engage the *Yūdachi* and the new assailant simultaneously. The searchlights went out, and the *Aaron Ward* ceased firing; so did her targets. The respite was brief. Less than a minute later, a brilliant set of starshells illuminated the destroyer and more shells landed around her. Gregor ordered flank speed to get away. Within ten minutes the *Aaron Ward* would lose steering control; ten minutes after that, she lost power.

The *Cushing* was in a similar situation. Seriously damaged after her close encounter with the *Hiei*, the crew of Stokes's flagship fought fires and made repairs. Lieutenant Commander Parker desperately wanted to get under way. In the meantime, the Japanese cruiser *Nagara* was leading a small task force through the combat zone. The *Amatsukaze* had dropped out of formation, but the *Yukikaze* resumed her position astern of the cruiser and the *Teruzuki* moved up to seal the gap. Together, these three ships came across the crippled *Cushing*: "A three stack Japanese light cruiser illuminated the ship from the starboard side and opened fire at a range of about 2000 yards. A second Japanese ship (probably a destroyer) also opened fire on the ship from the starboard quarter." With only 20-mm guns available to respond, Parker ordered his crew to abandon ship. The three Japanese ships turned off their lights and disappeared into the darkness.

Some distance to the west, Hoover's *Helena* was still seeking targets of opportunity. While the main and secondary batteries engaged the *Hiei* and the *Amatsukaze*, another target was sighted just 3,000 yards away. The forward starboard 40-mm mount opened fire, peppering the enemy bridge with high explosive. This target was most likely the *Kirishima*. She responded with her 14-inch guns. Two massive shells hit the *Helena*. One slammed into the face of Turret 4, just below the center gun. It dished in the turret face plate and scoured the gun barrels with shrapnel, but the turret remained in action. Another exploded on the deck near Turret 1. Hoover got out of the close-range melee and reengaged from longer range. She fired at her next target from beyond 16,000 yards.

In the meantime, Lieutenant Commander McCoombs took his destroyer *Monssen* north. She had followed the *Aaron Ward*, but the two destroyers became separated in the darkness. McCoombs sighted what appeared to be a Japanese destroyer with two white bands on her funnels. One of the stern 5-inch guns and some

The *Sterett* Fires on the *Yūdachi*

With a single roar our four guns spoke together. Four tracers sped straight and true to the target and exploded in her bridge structure. Five seconds later we fired our second salvo, and four more tracers leapt across the intervening 800 yards. We could not miss, and we did not. I noted with admiration how beautifully the tracers, which were probably some 300 feet apart when they started out from our gun muzzles, converged into a grouping no more than ten feet apart when they struck their target. Those four shells disappeared directly into the housings of the ship's after gun mounts. With a sudden, tremendous roar, she blew up. Her stern came completely out of the water, explosions obscured her after gun mounts, and a tremendous fireball burst skyward. As she settled back into the water, it looked as if the whole after section of her hull was cherry red. Involuntarily, I cried out, "Oh, you poor son of a bitch!" The water around her seemed to boil, and her hull threw off steam with a hiss that we could hear aboard the *Sterett*. I described the scene to the gun captains and told them to send their powder monkeys up the ladder to the main deck so they could see what they had just done. A few seconds later I heard their shouts and cheers as they viewed their vanquished foe. She burned brilliantly for a few minutes while we steamed past her; then there was total darkness.

—C. RAYMOND CALHOUN, *TIN CAN SAILOR: LIFE ABOARD THE USS* STERETT, *1939–1945*

of the automatic weapons opened fire as she passed to starboard. McCoombs kept on, expecting that there might be Japanese transports farther ahead. Instead, he was ambushed by the *Nagara*'s three-ship formation. They illuminated the *Monssen* with a starshell. Believing it had come from a friendly ship, McCoombs turned on his fighting lights. They became a focal point for two searchlight beams, a hail of Japanese shells, and four torpedoes. McCoombs avoided two torpedoes; the others passed under the *Monssen*'s hull. Shells knocked out both forward 5-inch guns, disabled the director, and cut down the men manning the rear guns. McCoombs called for flank speed, but hits to the machinery spaces had ruptured the steam lines. Survivors attempted to fight the fires, but with a ruptured fire main and no power, the situation was hopeless. Fearing the magazines might explode, and hoping to prevent further loss of life, McCoombs abandoned ship.

Rear Admiral Takama's destroyers, the *Asagumo*, *Murasame*, and *Samidare*, were north of the chaotic battle. When the fighting started, Takama accelerated to flank speed and began to look for targets of opportunity. His flagship *Asagumo* sighted the *Helena* and opened fire. His flag captain, Commander Toru Iwahashi, launched a salvo of torpedoes and claimed a series of hits, mistaking the rapid fire of the cruiser's 6-inch guns for a "great fire" and explosions.

Commander Naoji Suenaga's *Murasame* was next astern. He ordered his guns to open fire using searchlight illumination. The light settled on the *Juneau*'s bridge at about the same time the first 5-inch shells arrived. One torpedo out of a full salvo of eight also hit. It slammed into the forward fire room, killing everyone there, and disrupting power to the forward part of the ship. The suddenness of the *Murasame*'s attack took the *Juneau*'s crew by surprise. They had been firing at the destroyer *Yūdachi*. Fire control systems were knocked out. Shells crashed into the bridge, superstructure, and hull; Captain Swenson tried to get the crippled *Juneau* to safety. He aimed for Malaita Island, hoping to find a sheltered cove where his crew could perform repairs.

In the exchange, the *Murasame* was hit in the forward fire room, forcing Suenaga to take evasive action and turn off her searchlight, but the damage was slight. Suenaga took his ship north, away from the battle. Behind her, Commander Noboru Nakamura and his destroyer *Samidare* were having trouble finding targets. He ordered the torpedo battery trained out to engage an enemy ship, but the lookouts recognized her as the *Hiei*. The Japanese flagship was also having trouble separating friends from enemies. She fired on the *Samidare*. Nakamura turned on his recognition lights and the firing ceased. Then he saw the *Juneau* in the *Murasame*'s searchlight beam and opened fire. More 5-inch shells hit the cruiser, but she appeared to sink before Nakamura's crew could fire torpedoes. He turned the *Samidare* to follow in wake of the *Asagumo*.

As the two destroyers headed northeast, they ran across Lieutenant Commander Hank's *Laffey*. After his close-range duel with the *Hiei*, Hank had been using the backdrop of Savo Island to conceal his movements. He spotted the two Japanese destroyers approaching from about 3,000 yards. The *Samidare* passed ahead. Hank trained his guns on the *Asagumo*. A searchlight from Nakamura's ship illuminated the *Laffey*, and all three ships started shooting. Hits cut the power to the *Laffey*'s director, and the guns went to local control. The two stern mounts were knocked out. Mount 2 was hit. Only the foremost gun remained in action. The *Laffey* was unable to hit either of her assailants.

Samidare's searchlight gave the *Kirishima* a point of aim. Near misses from her main guns kicked up

The cruiser *Juneau* in New York Harbor on 11 February 1942. Note the many 5-inch gun turrets and her intricate camouflage scheme. The *Juneau* was hit by a torpedo the night of 12–13 November but survived to begin the voyage back to Espiritu Santo. That morning, the *Juneau* was hit by a torpedo from the submarine *I-26*; the cruiser exploded and disappeared. Although more than a hundred men survived the sinking, the remaining ships, wary of follow-up submarine attacks, did not stop. Only ten men were ultimately rescued. (National Archives)

The destroyer *Asagumo*, Rear Admiral Tamotsu Takama's flagship during the First Naval Battle of Guadalcanal. Along with the destroyer *Samidare*, the *Asagumo* crippled the destroyer *Laffey* and helped to sink her. (U.S. Naval Institute Photo Archive)

huge fountains of water that drenched the *Laffey* and knocked men to the deck. One shell passed through the superstructure amidships but failed to explode. Another hit the forward engine room. The cruiser *Nagara* passed close aboard, illuminating the destroyer with another searchlight and firing automatic weapons at her superstructure. A torpedo slammed into the *Laffey*'s stern, wrecking the fantail, bending propeller shafts, and starting a large fire. In the confusion, the *Samidare* and *Asagumo* lost contact with each other. The *Kirishima* and *Nagara* moved on, leaving the *Laffey* crippled. Although the fire died down, it flared back up with a vengeance after 0200. Hank ordered the *Laffey* abandoned; she sank at about 0220.

Some 20 minutes after almost firing on the *Aaron Ward*, Commander Coward and the *Sterett* approached another potential target. He was confident that this was an enemy vessel, so Coward approached cautiously. It was Commander Kikkawa's *Yūdachi*. Kikkawa had mistaken the *Sterett* for a friendly ship and turned on his recognition lights. Lieutenant Calhoun opened fire.

Shells hit the director, bridge, forward engine room, and number three fire room. *Yūdachi*'s engineering officers were immediately killed. Two torpedoes followed Calhoun's barrage. These appeared to explode and "lift the target out of the water," but neither of the torpedoes hit. Like so many others, Commander Coward and his men saw what they expected to see. They assumed the *Yudachi* was sinking as they retreated into the gloom and withdrew from the battle.

The last ship in the U.S. line was Commander Cole's *Fletcher*. Coached through the battle by Lieutenant Commander Wylie's effective use of the SG radar's PPI display, Cole tried to keep his ship from being ambushed as the American column "disintegrated." He cut a path through the enemy formation, made smoke, and fired at "random" targets. Fifteen minutes after the shooting started, Cole observed that "the general firing became sporadic, seeming to consist of individual duels." After making a long-range torpedo attack on the struggling *Hiei*, Cole took the *Fletcher* out of the sound through Sealark Channel.

The *Fletcher* was the last ship in Callaghan's long column. The destroyer is pictured here off New York on 18 July 1942. Her captain, Commander William Cole, and her executive officer, Lieutenant Commander Joe Wylie, worked out an effective technique for using the ship's SG radar that was a forerunner of the Navy's Combat Information Center (CIC). (National Archives)

AFTERMATH

AT ABOUT 0207, WITH ISOLATED BATTLES STILL GOING ON AROUND HIM, Captain Hoover tried to raise Admiral Callaghan and the flagship. "What is course?" he asked. When a second query failed to elicit a response, he tried to raise Captain DuBose on board the *Portland*: "What is course?" DuBose was still alive, but with the *Portland*'s radio out, he could not respond. Finally, Hoover broadcast a message to the entire formation: "Can you hear me?" Lieutenant Commander McCombs of the *Monssen* was the only one to reply. Hoover appeared to be the senior surviving officer, so he took command. He ordered the remaining ships of TG 67.4 to "Form 18, course 092, speed 18. Don't answer." As the *Helena* withdrew, the *Sterett* joined her. An unfamiliar ship

A ghostly *San Francisco* returns home and passes under the Golden Gate Bridge on a foggy day in December 1942. Heading to the Mare Island Navy Yard for repairs, she bears the scars of 12–13 November. (National Archives)

approached them, and Hoover challenged her by blinker light. She was the badly damaged *San Francisco*. McCandless responded in plain English: "Admiral Callaghan and Captain Young killed. Ship badly damaged. Take charge." Hoover did. The *Fletcher*, *O'Bannon*, and *Juneau* also joined up. These six ships exited Ironbottom Sound and began to make their way south.

The Japanese formation had also disintegrated. Although small task groups—like the one led by Rear Admiral Kimura—retained some cohesion, they eventually broke down in the melee. Vice Admiral Abe's flagship *Hiei* was seriously damaged, on fire, and barely under control. He had suffered a concussion and was unable to communicate with his ships in the darkness. The *Akatsuki* had been sunk, the *Yūdachi* was crippled, and the damaged destroyers *Amatsukaze* and *Ikazuchi* were retiring to the north. Captain Iwabuchi of the *Kirishima* considered an attack on the airfield but decided against it. He did not have time to identify the necessary landmarks, perform the bombardment, and get out of range of U.S. aircraft before daybreak.

As the Japanese ships steamed out of the sound, Kimura noticed that the flagship was not with them. He took *Nagara* back into the sound to look for her. The *Hiei* was on the western side of Savo Island; she had been hit by more than 100 shells. One flooded the steering engine room, shorting the motor. Others had knocked out fire control for the secondary battery and destroyed three of the guns. Fires were burning amidships. Half a dozen hits along the water line were letting water into the ship, and with several of the pumping motors disabled, it was difficult to correct the list that was developing. By 0500, she was pointed north, but almost dead in the water. Captain Nishida and his crew worked furiously to repair the damage. Kimura kept the *Nagara* nearby to offer what help he could and maintain communication between Abe and the rest of the formation. The Combined Fleet Staff quickly learned that the bombardment mission had failed. Admiral Ugaki recorded in his diary:

After sending its scheduled time of commencing bombardment on the enemy airfield at 0145, the dauntless

The *San Francisco* under repair at Mare Island on 15 December 1942. The white circles identify hits on her superstructure. Note the numerous shrapnel holes in her stack. (National Archives)

attack force encountered several enemy cruisers and ten destroyers at 0150. Through poor visibility, our destroyers fought with torpedo and gun fire at the range of 1500 to 800 meters. . . . Fire broke out near battleship *Hiei*'s bridge and her communication was interrupted. Under these circumstances, it was considered unfavorable to carry out today's convoy transportation, so an order was issued to postpone its date to the 14th.

—13 NOVEMBER 1942, FROM *FADING VICTORY: THE DIARY OF ADMIRAL MATOME UGAKI, 1941–1945* (NAVAL INSTITUTE PRESS, 2008)

Rear Admiral Callaghan's gamble paid off; he had thwarted the bombardment of Henderson Field and forced Rear Admiral Tanaka's transport force to withdraw back to the Shortlands. But TG 67.4 was decimated in what became known as the First Naval Battle of Guadalcanal. As the *San Francisco* headed south, Lieutenant Commander Schonland requested medical assistance; more than 100 wounded men, including Captain Young (mistakenly reported as killed), were fighting to survive on board the flagship. The ship's medical staff was overwhelmed. After sunrise, Dr. Malcom M. Dunham and two pharmacist's mates came over from the *O'Bannon*. The *Juneau* also sent a contingent led by Dr. Roger O'Neil. As soon as O'Neil boarded the flagship, he joined the attempt to save Captain Young's life.

Hoover assumed an unusual formation. The *Helena* led the cruisers; the *San Francisco* followed in her wake. The *Juneau* had difficulty maneuvering, so to minimize the risk of collision, she steamed 800 yards on the *San Francisco*'s starboard quarter. The *Sterett* and *Fletcher* formed an antisubmarine screen, flanking the bows of the *Helena*. Because her sonar equipment was damaged, the *O'Bannon* was sent ahead to radio details of the battle to Admiral Halsey. Aware that there were enemy submarines in the area, Hoover zigzagged to present a more difficult target.

At 1100, his ships were sighted by Commander Minoru Yokota in submarine *I-26*. He suspected there was a U.S. formation in the area, so, at about 1030, he took his boat down to 40 meters, stopped the engines, and listened for contacts. He followed the sound of Hoover's ships and sighted them when he returned to periscope depth. Yokota approached cautiously and fired two torpedoes at the *San Francisco* before diving to 70 meters. Lookouts on board the crippled cruiser sighted the approaching torpedoes; she took evasive action. One torpedo passed ahead. Its course took it straight into the *Juneau*.

When the torpedo hit there was a large single explosion and the air was filled with debris, much of it in large pieces. There appeared to be no distinct series of small explosions and the whole ship disappeared in a large cloud of black, yellow black, and brown smoke. Debris showered down among ships of the formation for several minutes after the explosion.

—CAPTAIN GILBERT C. HOOVER, USS *HELENA*, 14 NOVEMBER 1942

Hoover quickly considered his options. His destroyers had failed to detect the approaching submarine, calling into question their ability to prevent another attack. The *San Francisco* was crippled and full of wounded men. Hoover increased speed and left the area, leaving Captain Swenson—a U.S. Naval Academy classmate and personal friend—and the other survivors of the *Juneau* in the water. Hoping for a quick rescue, Hoover transmitted details of the sinking to a B-17 overhead. He expected the bomber's crew to forward the message to Halsey's command, but the pilot, believing he could only break radio silence if he sighted enemy ships, failed to pass it on. Halsey learned of the *Juneau*'s loss when Hoover returned to Espiritu Santo the next day. For abandoning the survivors, Halsey relieved Hoover of his command; he served the remainder of the war in the Bureau of Ordnance.

More than 100 survivors of the *Juneau* clung to life jackets and rafts. They would not be rescued for eight days; by then, only ten were still alive. Among the missing were the five sons of Thomas and Aletta Sullivan of Waterloo, Iowa. George, Frank, Joe, Matt, and Al had enlisted in January 1942 and resolved to serve together. The family's five gold stars became a rallying point for the nation, and they lent their name to a new ship, the destroyer *Sullivans* (DD-537), commissioned in September 1943.

THE CRIPPLES

Back in Ironbottom Sound, the sun rose on a collection of crippled ships. The *Portland* was still circling. Captain DuBose was afraid of being torpedoed by Japanese submarines, so he maintained speed. The *Atlanta* was slowly drifting toward Guadalcanal. The abandoned *Cushing* continued to burn; the *Monssen* was in a similar state, but sharks in the water convinced three of her crew to return to the ship. The *Aaron Ward*, with her crew still on board, was farthest to the north. West of her was the crippled *Yūdachi*, drifting with the tide,

Among the missing from the loss of the *Juneau* were the five Sullivan brothers of Waterloo, Iowa. They are pictured here during the ship's commissioning ceremonies on 14 February 1942. They are (left to right) Joseph ("Joe"), Francis ("Frank"), Albert ("Al"), Madison ("Matt"), and George. (Naval History and Heritage Command)

still burning, and abandoned. Captain DuBose made sure of her identity and then opened fire: "At 0630 after positively identifying the *Shigure* class destroyer, we opened fire on it, range 12,500 yards. Six 6-gun salvoes were fired, she was hit several times, and when the sixth salvo landed her after magazines blew . . . and she sank immediately."

The men on board the *Atlanta* cheered. Commander Gregor of the *Aaron Ward* tried not to suffer a similar fate. The tug *Bobolink* (AT-131) had come out from the anchorage at Tulagi to assist her, and at about 0620, a line was secured. The battleship *Hiei*, crippled but still full of fight, saw the two ships and opened fire. The fourth salvo straddled the destroyer. Gregor decided ruining his boilers with salt water was an acceptable trade for preserving his ship. He worked up to speed, cast off the tow cable, and dodged incoming shells on his way to safety at Tulagi. The *Hiei* quickly became distracted by American planes.

The *Bobolink* proceeded to the *Atlanta*, while a small fleet of landing craft rescued men from the water and took them off the damaged ships. The *Monssen* blew up and sank at about noon. By 1400, the *Atlanta*

had taken on so much water that further towing was impossible. With her anchor grounded off Lunga Point, she wallowed on the tide. Captain Jenkins decided to scuttle the *Atlanta*, and she went down at about 2015. Three hours before, the *Cushing*, which had been burning throughout the day, finally sank. The *Bobolink* moved on to help the *Portland*. Her shattered stern made it extremely difficult to steam in a straight line. Together with YP-239, the *Bobolink* managed to keep her moving, but progress was slow, and night fell while she was still in the sound. The cruiser was not safe in Tulagi Harbor until 0130 the next morning.

THE *HIEI* SCUTTLED

In the meantime, aviators from Henderson Field did their best to finish what Rear Admiral Callaghan had started. Before dawn seven dive bombers took off on scouting missions; three more were sent on a "special tracking mission" to locate wounded Japanese ships. They found the *Hiei* north of Savo Island, circling at low speed. Her rudder was jammed. The destroyer *Yukikaze* was nearby, watching over the crippled flagship. Twenty miles beyond, they found the *Kirishima* and escorting destroyers.

The Loss of the *Hiei*

Immediately after the commencement of fighting, enemy gunfire was concentrated on *Hiei*. More than fifty shells, as well as numerous machine-gun bullets, hit the foremast, antiaircraft guns, machine guns, searchlight, and other structures. Gun firing became impossible for the time being, as the electric circuit of the main battery system and the control tower of the secondary battery were damaged. Fires broke out at several spots near the foremast. Then the steering gear room was hit and flooded, rendering steering impossible. She then was navigated with the use of engines and reached a point west of Savo Island by 0600. But, as the rudder then stuck to one side, she eventually lost steering ability, so she circled in almost the same spot. . . . Under attacks from more than sixty torpedo planes and bombers coming from 0730 to 1230—three hits and numerous near misses—strenuous efforts were made to fight fire and flood. At 1430, when manual steering was made possible, after placing the fire at the foremast under control and the pumping of the flooded steering room proved effective, about twelve carrier torpedo planes came to attack her. Torpedoes hit the midship and stern on her starboard and the starboard engine room was flooded. Then water poured in from holes made in her side, and the listing increased. Pumping of the steering gear room became impossible, and engines could not be used because of flooding. Thereupon I ordered all hands to abandon ship and decided to sink her by our own hand. The transfer of her crew was completed by 1800.

—SUMMARY ACTION REPORT NO. 2, COMMANDER 11TH BATTLESHIP DIVISION, VICE ADMIRAL HIROAKE ABE, 14 NOVEMBER 1942, FROM *FADING VICTORY: THE DIARY OF ADMIRAL MATOME UGAKI, 1941–1945* (NAVAL INSTITUTE PRESS, 2008)

Between the two battleships, there were four destroyers—the *Teruzuki* leading Captain Setoyama's Destroyer Division 27 with the *Shigure*, *Shiratsuyu*, and *Yugure*—approaching the *Hiei* to take off survivors.

At Henderson Field, Brigadier General Woods worked to ensure the destruction of the Japanese battleship. The first strike took off at 0615 and attacked as the *Hiei* was firing at the *Aaron Ward*. One bomb struck the superstructure amidships; four others were close misses. Kinkaid committed the *Enterprise*'s planes to the effort, shuttling them to and from the airfields on Guadalcanal. Hundreds of miles to the north, Kondo ordered the carrier *Junyō* to cover Abe's retreating force. Eight Zeros took off at 0530 and headed south. They arrived just as a flight of torpedo bombers approached the *Hiei*. A fierce low-altitude dogfight developed between the Japanese fighters and escorting Wildcats while the torpedo bombers made their runs. The battleship fired her remaining antiaircraft guns, and even used incendiary-shrapnel rounds from her main battery. They kicked up large splashes around the torpedo bombers and sent pieces of metal flying through their wings. The pilots claimed two torpedo hits. After being sighted by reconnaissance planes, the *Junyō* retired; the *Hiei* struggled on as Woods kept up the pressure.

Another strike attacked at 0915. No bombs hit, but it looked like a torpedo did. About an hour later, a squadron of *Enterprise* torpedo bombers swept the sound. They approached the *Hiei* from both bows, in a classic "hammer and anvil" attack, claiming three hits. Strikes continued through the day. Dive bombers and torpedo bombers combined with B-17s from Espiritu Santo to pound the crippled battleship. That afternoon a large strike of 8 dive-bombers, 6 torpedo bombers, and 14 fighters set out from Henderson field. Heavy weather and low clouds spoiled the dive-bombing attack, but torpedo bombers made two hits (and claimed three). One struck the starboard side forward of the bridge. The second, dropped by Lieutenant (junior grade) George D. Welles, hit the same side farther aft, opening the starboard engine room to the sea. The damage put an end to Captain Nishida's repair efforts and doomed the *Hiei*. Abe gave the order to scuttle his flagship; 450 of the *Hiei*'s men went down with her.

CACTUS SURVIVES

On 13 November, Yamamoto's plans were in disarray. With the U.S. airbase still active, it was too dangerous for Tanaka's transports to approach. However, one part of the plan continued. Vice Admiral Mikawa was moving ahead with his bombardment mission. Originally, the plan assumed his attack would cover the transports as they unloaded that night. Instead, he would attempt to disable Henderson Field. Mikawa's efforts would be augmented by an impromptu follow-up the next night, led by Vice Admiral Kondō.

Mikawa's force skirted north of the islands of Choiseul and Santa Isabel to avoid detection. As it approached

Guadalcanal, it divided in two. A covering force with the heavy cruisers *Chōkai* and *Kinugasa*, light cruiser *Isuzu*, and two destroyers swept the waters of the sound, while the bombardment unit under Rear Admiral Shōji Nishimura headed toward Lunga Point. Nishimura's two heavy cruisers—the *Suzuya* and *Maya*—shelled the airfield for half an hour. Two fighters were set on fire. Three more fighters and a dive bomber were badly damaged; 31 fighters were lightly damaged. The bombardment was frustrating for the island's defenders, but the damage was much less than what Abe's battleships would have done.

Nishimura and Mikawa were able to attack unopposed because Halsey's last surface action group—TF 64 under Rear Admiral Willis A. Lee—was too far away to intervene. Lee was escorting Kinkaid's *Enterprise* task force, and the carrier's progress toward Guadalcanal that day had been interrupted by flight operations and emergency turns to avoid submarine contacts. When Halsey's orders to detach Lee arrived, the carrier group was still 350 miles from Ironbottom Sound. TF 64 was unable to make up the distance that night.

However, sufficient striking strength remained at Henderson Field to contest Mikawa's withdrawal. Morning searches found his ships, and a strike caught them near Rendova Island at about 0830. One of the dive bombers hit the cruiser *Kinugasa*, killing Captain Masao Sawa. Planes from the *Enterprise* attacked the *Kinugasa* later that day. They all missed, but their bombs fell close enough to do serious damage. The concussive force from near misses ruptured the hull, increasing the flooding and knocking out the steering gear. The cruiser sank at about 1120.

More planes from the *Enterprise* found Mikawa's remaining ships at 1015. Two near misses on the flagship *Chōkai* disrupted hull plates and flooded some compartments, but she could still make 29 knots. Near misses also damaged the *Isuzu*; water came into two of her firerooms and damaged her steering control, but she also kept going. Mikawa's bombardment had wrecked six planes and damaged 32 more for the cost of one cruiser sunk and two damaged.

Search planes from Henderson Field found the Japanese transports at about 0700 on 14 November. Rear Admiral Tanaka had departed the Shortlands the previous evening, hoping that Nishimura's bombardment would be enough to ensure safe passage the following day. The planes found them when they were north of New Georgia Island. About 0850, two search planes from the *Enterprise* also appeared over Tanaka's force. They made

ineffective attacks after sending their contact report. It would be the first of many strikes that day.

The weather over the Solomon Islands was clear, and attacking pilots had no difficulty finding Tanaka and his convoy. The first major strike came in around 1245. The *Canberra Maru* and *Nagara Maru* were hit by torpedoes and left in a sinking condition. The *Sado Maru* lost steering control from a bomb that exploded nearby. The rest of the ships were scattered after maneuvering individually to avoid the attacking planes. Tanaka dispatched two destroyers to rescue survivors and tend to the crippled *Sado Maru*. He continued on with nine destroyers and the eight remaining transports.

At 1305, another strike took off from the *Enterprise* and headed for the transports. While they were in the air, the second and third strikes from Henderson Field attacked Tanaka's ships. They claimed six hits. Soon thereafter, a flight of seven B-17s from Espirtu Santo attacked from 17,000 feet. Their spread of bombs bracketed one transport and evidently scored a hit. These strikes set fire to the *Brisbane Maru*; Tanaka dispatched the destroyer *Kawakaze* to take off survivors and kept going with his remaining ships.

The *Enterprise* strike found them at about 1500. Fighting their way through the escorting Zeros, the Dauntlesses dove on the transports. Both the *Shinanogawa Maru* and *Arizona Maru* were hit, set afire, and left sinking. Another flight of eight B-17s arrived and made an ineffective bombing run from 20,000 feet. The destroyers *Naganami* and *Makinami* stood by the crippled transports and evacuated survivors. One final strike attacked that evening. As the bombers and their escorts approached the transports, the skies above became "one mass dogfight." Escorting Zeros did their best, but bombs struck the *Nako Maru*, starting fires and setting off ammunition. She was hastily abandoned and left adrift.

The crews at Henderson Field worked relentlessly all day to refuel and rearm aircraft for these strikes on the transports. Even cooks and messmen were pressed into service, leaving the men little prepared food to eat that evening. But the results were impressive. Seven transports had been damaged or sunk; only four remained in the convoy approaching Guadalcanal. The bold efforts of Rear Admiral Callaghan and the men of TG 67.4 had thrown off Japanese plans and bought the aviators valuable time. But as the sun set over Henderson Field, one more test for the Navy's sailors remained.

BATTLESHIP DUEL

HALSEY KNEW HE HAD TO PROTECT THE AIRFIELDS FROM FURTHER BOMBARDMENT, so he sent Rear Admiral Lee's powerful TF 64 into Ironbottom Sound. Lee had two modern battleships, the *Washington* and *South Dakota*, escorted by the destroyers *Walke* (DD-416), *Benham* (DD-397), *Gwin*, and *Preston*. The destroyers were an impromptu formation; they were chosen because they had the most fuel remaining, not because they were a cohesive force. There was no senior destroyer commander, such as Stokes or Tobin, to coordinate their movements. To mitigate this weakness, Lee—known as "one of the best brains in the Navy"—developed an effective battle plan. As the ships approached Guadalcanal, he transmitted it to his captains.

Rear Admiral Willis A. Lee, pictured in 1942. Lee commanded Task Force 64, which thwarted a Japanese attempt to bombard Henderson Field at the Second Naval Battle of Guadalcanal. (Naval History and Heritage Command)

The four destroyers would operate ahead of the battleships. Lee refused to tie them to the battle line, explicitly rejecting the linear formation used by Scott and Callaghan. The battleships, with the flagship *Washington* in the lead, would follow about 5,000 yards behind. The destroyers would identify and flush out targets for the battleships' guns. Lee expected gunfire to be the decisive weapon; all ships were instructed to open fire as soon as a target presented itself.

Lee's emphasis on gunfire was natural; he was a gunnery expert. As a member of the 1920 U.S. Olympic team, he had won seven medals for marksmanship, five of them gold. Before the war, he had served as director of fleet training and became extremely familiar with the most effective procedures for accurate gunfire. He tempered this knowledge with a clear understanding of the strengths and limitations of radar. Under his direction, the *Washington*'s gunnery department had reached an extremely high level of proficiency; she was arguably the most accurate battleship in the fleet.

As skilled as Lee and his men were, the decision to send two of the Navy's most modern battleships into the narrow waters off Guadalcanal was a serious risk that violated established doctrine. Battleships had proven vulnerable in mock night combat before the war; in confused close-range actions, smaller ships could overwhelm their control positions with concentrated gunfire, just as Callaghan's ships had disabled the *Hiei*. The decision to send TF 64 into Ironbottom Sound was a calculated risk; Halsey committed Lee because he knew success in the campaign depended on preserving the planes, aviators, and supplies at Lunga Point.

While Lee was taking position, Vice Admiral Kondō's Emergency Bombardment Group approached. His mission was not part of the original plan, but after the failure of Abe's bombardment, something had to be done to damage the airfield and help ensure the survival of the transports. Kondō had the battleship *Kirishima* and the two heavy cruisers *Atago* and *Takao*. They were screened by Rear Admiral Susumu Kimura's light cruiser

The destroyer *Walke* at Mare Island in California on 24 August 1942. The circles indicate modifications made during her time in the yard; they include the addition of an FD radar set on her gun director. The *Walke* was the lead destroyer in Rear Admiral Lee's formation the night of 14 November 1942. (National Archives)

Nagara and six destroyers. A sweeping unit with three destroyers led by Rear Admiral Shintarō Hashimoto in the light cruiser *Sendai* would patrol ahead of Kondō's formation and identify any potential threats. From afar, Admiral Ugaki maintained a close eye on the proceedings:

> The advance force [under Vice Admiral Kondō], consisting of the flagship *Atago*, *Takao* with three destroyers, and battleship *Kirishima* with one cruiser and three destroyers, preceded by one cruiser and three destroyers, proceeded southward. They entered the Roads at 2330 from the west side of Savo Island and were to bombard the airfield while preparing for the enemy's counterattack on our convoy.
>
> A report of sighting two cruisers and four destroyers heading north at a point twenty miles west of Savo Island came in from a plane. Then we picked up an enemy telegram of "I am in action" at 2230. Thus a night battle has started as expected. How will it come out?

—14 NOVEMBER 1942, FROM *FADING VICTORY: THE DIARY OF ADMIRAL MATOME UGAKI, 1941–1945* (NAVAL INSTITUTE PRESS, 2008)

Lee had advance warning of Kondō's approach. Patrol planes sighted the Japanese formation the afternoon of the 14th, giving Lee time to prepare and anticipate Kondō's moves. Lee arrived off Guadalcanal that evening and swept the waters north of Savo Island before entering the sound. Unlike the action two nights before, the visibility in Ironbottom Sound the night of 14 November was relatively good. Lieutenant W. J. Collum Jr., on board the *Walke*, noted that there was a half moon and "the sea was flat calm." Other ships reported similar conditions. The good visibility would help lookouts spot targets at longer ranges.

CHAOS AMONG THE SCREENS

First contact came soon after 2300. Lee, with his formation well into the heart of the sound, was on a westerly course. The SG radars on board the battleships detected Hashimoto's sweeping unit to the east of Savo Island, and lookouts quickly spotted the Japanese ships.

> At 2308 three ships were observed from the bridge visually, and checked by radar to bear 330 degrees true, range 18,100 yards. The leading ship was large and is believed to have been a heavy cruiser or a battleship. Astern of it were two smaller ships, believed to be light cruisers, possibly one of them being

Vice Admiral Nobutake Kondō. He commanded the Japanese Emergency Bombardment Group at the Second Naval Battle of Guadalcanal. He had previously commanded the main Japanese formations in the Guadalcanal Campaign, including those at the Battle of the Eastern Solomons and the Battle of the Santa Cruz Islands. (Naval History and Heritage Command)

a heavy cruiser. Contact was reported by TBS to the task force commander, and he very soon after this ordered "open fire when you are ready."

—CAPTAIN THOMAS L. GATCH, USS *SOUTH DAKOTA*, 24 NOVEMBER 1942

The *Sendai* and her accompanying destroyers, the *Shikinami* and *Uranami*, had been mistaken for much larger ships. Once the *Washington* and *South Dakota* brought their guns onto the targets, they opened fire.

> Main battery opened fire on target at a range of 18,500 yards. Secondary battery opened fire on closer targets possibly destroyers, groups One and Three firing (two mounts each). Probably about 15,000 yards range, possibly less. Secondary battery Group One officer stated that there appeared to be three destroyers in the group at which he fired.

—CAPTAIN GLENN B. DAVIS, USS *WASHINGTON*, 27 NOVEMBER 1942

The initial salvoes from the *South Dakota*'s stern turret ignited fires among her scout planes on the aft deck, illuminating the ship, but the blast from subsequent

The Night Action of 14–15 November 1942

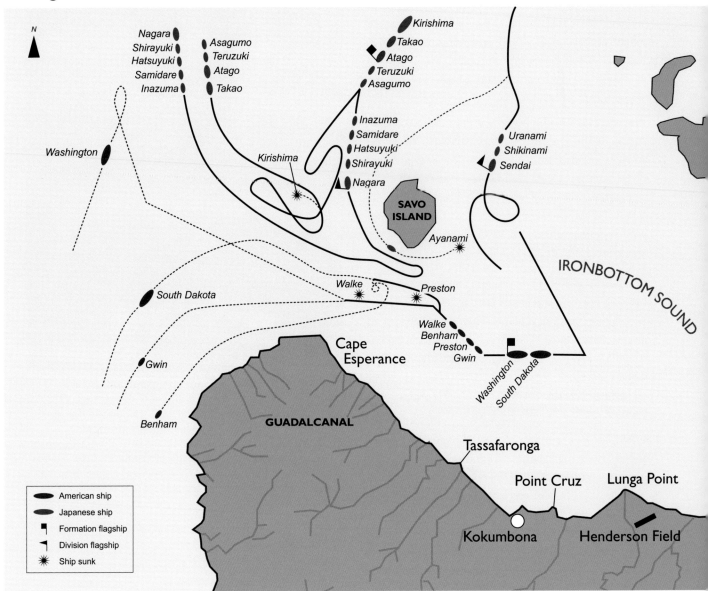

Order of Battle: 14–15 November 1942

**Navy Forces -
Rear Admiral Willis A. Lee**

Destroyers
Walke
(Commander Thomas M. Stokes)
Benham
Preston
Gwin

Battleships
Washington (flag)
South Dakota

**IJN Forces -
Vice Admiral Nobutake Kondō**

Bombardment Unit
Atago (flag)
Takao
Kirishima

Screen
Nagara
(Rear Admiral Susumu Kimura)
Shirayuki
Hatsuyuki
Samidare

Screen cont.
Inazuma
Asagumo
Teruzuki

Sweeping Unit
Sendai
(Rear Admiral Shintaro Hashimoto)
Shikinami
Uranami
Ayanami

UNITED STATES NAVAL INSTITUTE

The light cruiser *Sendai*, flagship of Rear Admiral Hashimoto's sweeping unit. The *Sendai* was typical of IJN light cruisers built soon after World War I. She maneuvered to avoid the gunfire of the *Washington* and *South Dakota* at the Second Naval Battle of Guadalcanal but succumbed to the combined fire of four U.S. Navy cruisers a year later at the Battle of Empress Augusta Bay. (U.S. Naval Institute Photo Archive)

salvoes blew the burning planes overboard. "Hits" were observed on the target, and her commanding officer, Captain Thomas L. Gatch, reported that the "initial salvoes started fires." This was wishful thinking. No hits were scored on the *Sendai* and her consorts. Hashimoto laid a smokescreen and used it to obscure his withdrawal. As the *Sendai, Shikinami,* and *Uranami* disappeared from sight and radar screens, the *Washington's* gunners believed they had sunk their first target.

In the meantime, Hashimoto's third destroyer, the *Ayanami*, was sweeping around the western side of Savo Island. She had been sent to scout the other entrance to the sound ahead of Kondō's main body. The Japanese destroyer hugged the shoreline, making her nearly invisible to lookouts and radars. Behind her was Kimura's screening unit. Commander Thomas E. Fraser, captain of the *Walke*, was at the front of Lee's formation. His fire control radar picked them up, and his gunners opened fire while he increased speed to 26 knots.

At 2330 the *Walke* made contact with FD radar on enemy ships on starboard beam; range about 15,000 yards, and opened fire immediately thereafter with 5-in battery. At 2332 the *Preston* opened fire on targets bearing about 045 degrees relative in vicinity of southeastern portion of Savo Island. The *Walke* shifted fire to these targets, believed to have been cruisers and destroyers; range about 7500 yards. These enemy ships returned fire and splashes were observed to fall short in the water on starboard side. Shortly thereafter a fire broke out on one of the enemy ships. At 2334 an enemy ship (probable a heavy cruiser) bearing about 280 degrees relative, opened fire. The *Walke* immediately shifted fire to this target; range about 5000 yards. This enemy ship had apparently steamed around Cape Esperance close aboard from westward, and was headed eastward along the shoreline of Guadalcanal Island. With enemy ships firing from both sides, many splashes were observed to fall all around the ship.

—LIEUTENANT W. J. COLLUM JR., USS *WALKE*, 30 NOVEMBER 1942

A confused battle broke out between Lee's destroyers and Kimura's screening unit. The *Ayanami* did her best to remain concealed; she fired a torpedo salvo and then

The destroyer *Ayanami* as completed in the early 1930s. She has three 5-inch twin mounts and three triple 24-inch torpedo mounts. Part of Rear Admiral Hashimoto's sweeping unit, the *Ayanami* found herself in a running battle with Rear Admiral Lee's destroyers. She launched a deadly salvo of torpedoes but was left crippled and burning. When the flames reached her torpedo battery, she exploded and sank. (U.S. Naval Institute Photo Archive)

A sharp image of the destroyer *Benham*, taken off the Mare Island Navy Yard on 6 February 1942. She was crippled in the night action of 14–15 November 1942 and scuttled the next day. (Naval History and Heritage Command)

reversed course away from the action. The specific identity of the "heavy cruiser" *Walke* engaged is unknown. Kondō's heavy cruisers were northeast of Savo at that point, and no other Japanese ships appear to have been on the port side of the U.S. line. However, two of Lee's other destroyers described an enemy cruiser on the port quarter. They might have misidentified the battleship *Washington*. She was 5,000 yards away on a similar bearing and, when her secondary battery opened fire to support the destroyers, one turret fired on an incorrect bearing. It might have hit the American destroyers.

Astern of the *Walke*, Lieutenant Commander John B. Taylor's *Benham* opened fire. Her men were unable to precisely identify Kimura's ships against the gloom and aimed at the dull flashes of enemy guns, using SC radar to determine the range. From the number and arrangement of the flashes, Taylor thought he was firing at a destroyer, so he withheld torpedoes, hoping to find a larger target. At 2338, the *Benham* was rocked by a tremendous explosion. A torpedo—most likely from the *Ayanami's* salvo—slammed into the forward part of the ship; it ripped off part of the hull and kicked up a huge column of water, drenching the destroyer amidships and sweeping one man overboard. The shattered hull acted like a brake, rapidly decelerating the ship to about five knots.

The *Preston* was the next destroyer in line. Commander Max C. Stormes sighted a Japanese destroyer in the moonlight and opened fire, quickly establishing the "hitting range." When this ship began to "burn fiercely," Stormes shifted to a second target; the *Preston* and Kimura's flagship *Nagara* engaged in

A Torpedo Hits the *Benham*

When astern of *Walke*, *Benham* came right and continued on the base course. . . . At 2338 *Benham* was hit by a torpedo on the starboard side at about frame six. The ship rose forward about four feet, heeled about five degrees to port, then rolled to starboard about thirty degrees, settling by the head and righting slowly. Speed through the water was decelerated in a very brief interval from twenty-seven knots to five knots or less. It is believed that this sudden deceleration contributed largely to the buckling of hull plating and longitudinals later discovered. The explosion threw up a tremendous volume of hot water which rose some twenty feet higher than the director and descended about the entire ship with considerable force. The after part of the ship settled momentarily so that the crew of Gun 4 were waist deep in water. This descending water, or water coming aboard over the deck edge when the stern settled, caused all the serious injuries to personnel in the vicinity of the tubes, and carried one man overboard. About this same time the *Preston* was hit, presumably by a torpedo, and blew up. A considerable quantity of water, oil, and debris from *Preston* fell on *Benham* aft, shortly after the water from our hit.

—LIEUTENANT COMMANDER JOHN B. TAYLOR, USS *BENHAM*, 29 NOVEMBER 1942

a running gun battle. Just after 2335, two shells from the light cruiser (mistaken for 6-inch) hit the *Preston* amidships. The explosions wrecked her firerooms and started fires within the torpedo battery. Another salvo of shells hit a moment later; these apparently came from the port side and were estimated as 8-inch. They wrecked the after part of the ship, knocking out the aft guns and igniting ammunition. From the *Walke*, it looked like the *Preston* had exploded.

At 2335 the *Preston* was hit on her port side, presumably by the enemy cruiser to port. The *Preston* seemed to sheer out to starboard, blowing up and sinking immediately. Shortly thereafter, an enemy cruiser was sighted ahead in direction of Savo Island, on course approximately 020 degrees true. This ship opened fire and salvoes [from it] . . . were observed both over and short, all slightly to starboard. The *Walke* immediately shifted the fire of the forward group to this target bearing 020 degrees relative; range about 7000 yards, at the same time maintaining fire on the cruisers to port with the after group. Speed was changed to twenty-six knots. The *Benham* sheered out to port; reason unknown. The enemy cruiser ahead disappeared behind Savo Island, at which time the *Walke* shifted fire to the enemy ships in vicinity of southern portion of Savo Island.

—LIEUTENANT W. J. COLLUM JR., USS *WALKE*, 30 NOVEMBER 1942

The Preston was mortally wounded and sinking; Commander Stormes would order his crew to abandon ship just after the devastating salvo. Moments after the *Preston* was hit, a torpedo struck the *Walke* forward of the bridge. It sheared off the destroyer's bow and ignited her forward magazine. Part of the bow, still afloat, drifted away as the *Walke* burned. She quickly settled in the water and started sinking.

The *Gwin* was the last of Lee's destroyers still in action. Her captain, Lieutenant Commander John B. Fellows Jr., had been engaging Kimura's destroyers, but like Taylor, had trouble discerning them against the backdrop of Salvo Island. As Fellows observed the *Preston* "explode," a shell hit the *Gwin's* number 2 engine room. Shrapnel tore through the ship and the surrounding compartments filled with steam; the explosion knocked three torpedoes out of their mount and over the side. An underwater explosion—Fellows attributed it to the *Preston's* depth charges, but it was more likely the *Walke's* magazine exploding—shook the *Gwin's* hull as she passed by the *Preston*. A few minutes later, a torpedo narrowly missed the *Gwin's* stern, passing within just 30 yards.

At 2348, Lee ordered his destroyers to retire. The *Gwin* was the only one that could comply; she was

The *Preston* Is Crippled

At about 2330 a ship was sighted off the southern tip of Savo Island and on the starboard bow of the *Preston*. Fire was opened immediately with all four guns bearing on the enemy ship which appeared to be a heavy destroyer or a light cruiser. Starshells were not used because the target was seen quite plainly in the moonlight. The range was estimated at 9000 yards and salvoes spotted to the target. The hitting range was established after only a few salvoes and the fire was very effective. The battery was in automatic control using director fire. The enemy ship moved into the shadow of Savo Island but she could still be distinguished and fire on her was continued. Approximately a minute after the *Preston* opened fire the enemy ship returned fire with her main battery plus what appeared to be 40-mm guns. At 2335 this ship caught fire and began to burn fiercely. At about the same time we observed that the ship that one of the battleships had been firing on caught fire also. Fire from the *Preston* was shifted to another ship in the shadow of Savo Island at a range of about 8000 yards. At 2335 ½ the *Preston* was hit on the starboard side by two projectiles, probably 6-in. One projectile hit between the two fire rooms killing all men in them and covering the amidships area with firebrick and debris.

A few seconds after the *Preston* was hit on the starboard side she was hit on the port side by part of a salvo of 8-in shells. As near as can be determined the ship was hit by three projectiles. The whole after part of the ship from the stacks aft was a mass of blazing, red-hot wreckage. One projectile hit in the engine room exploding after it hit the generators. A second projectile hit between the secondary control station and Number 3 gun. The third projectile hit Number 4 gun. Almost every man aft of the after machine gun nest was killed, including the executive officer. The gunnery officer gave the order for Guns 1 and 2 to continue firing if possible but the force of the explosion had jammed them both in train and elevation and they could not fire. The ship immediately listed sharply to starboard and began to settle by the stern. At 2336, the Commanding Officer, Commander M. C. Stormes, gave the order to abandon ship. In less than half a minute the ship rolled over on its side and sank by the stern.

—LIEUTENANT (JUNIOR GRADE) W. W. WOODS, USS *PRESTON*, 30 NOVEMBER 1942

A prewar picture of the destroyer *Gwin*, taken in 1941. She is pictured without radar and with very little antiaircraft armament. Note the lack of gunhouses on two of her 5-inch guns. (Naval History and Heritage Command)

damaged but would survive. Later that morning, she returned to scuttle her crippled companion, the *Benham*. Lee's destroyers had sacrificed themselves to flush out enemy targets, much as Lee had planned. But they had also done damage; the *Ayanami*, which had launched a volley of deadly torpedoes, was crippled and on fire. The fires spread to the oxygen tanks in her torpedo battery, triggering an explosion that broke her in two.

CONTEST OF GIANTS

While the destroyers were embroiled in their desperate struggle, the *South Dakota* experienced a debilitating power failure. A short caused the breakers on her main switchboard to trip and knocked out all power to her fire control systems. When power was routed to a secondary board, those breakers also tripped. Her crew desperately struggled to bring the power back on. They found the problem and isolated the problematic circuit—it involved two mounts in the secondary battery—within two minutes. Power was back on by 2335, but those two minutes were very costly.

Captain Glenn B. Davis steered his battleship *Washington* around the damaged destroyers, putting their burning hulls between him and the enemy and keeping the flagship obscured in the darkness behind the flames. When the power went out on board the *South Dakota*, Captain Gatch lost situational awareness. Although he initially moved to port to avoid the burning destroyers, he came around to starboard to clear them. When he did so, the *South Dakota* was silhouetted against their fires and clearly visible to the Japanese. As the

The destroyer *Smith* at the Mare Island Navy Yard on 21 September 1936. She had been commissioned two days before. Her sister ship, the *Preston*, is astern. She is still being fitted out. The *Preston* was the fourth destroyer in Rear Admiral Lee's force at the Second Naval Battle of Guadalcanal and was sunk in a close-range fight with Japanese screening forces. (National Archives)

An overhead view of the battleship *South Dakota*, taken at Nouméa, New Caledonia, in November 1942. The repair ship *Prometheus* is alongside; the destroyers are most likely *Mahan* (showing damage to her bow from a collision with the battleship) and *Lamson*. The *South Dakota* was disabled by electrical failures and subjected to a heavy fire at the Second Naval Battle of Guadalcanal. Prompt action by the *Washington* saved her from more serious damage. (National Archives)

The *Walke* Mortally Wounded

The *Walke* was hit by a partial salvo of 8-in shells and by a torpedo; the partial salvo coming from a cruiser from the vicinity of the southern portion of Savo Island, and the torpedo—according to observed track—coming from an unobserved enemy vessel (believed later to have been a submarine) on the starboard beam. When the torpedo hit just forward of the bridge, the ship was lifted bodily out of the water forward with great shock. All lights and communications failed immediately. The bow was broken off completely just forward of the

bridge superstructure, and this separate portion of the ship floated away—the bow was still floating when observed several days later. The ship turned slowly to port, going down by the bow. Fires broke out throughout the ship and were soon blazing fiercely from stem to stern. Number 2 magazine exploded with the initial impact of the torpedo, rupturing the forward fuel oil tanks and tearing great holes in the superstructure decks, including the director deck. The main deck was awash with several inches of fuel oil. Ready service stowages of

both 5-in and 20-mm ammunition began blowing up. At 2343 the Commanding Officer, Commander Thomas E. Fraser, U.S. Navy, upon seeing that the ship was burning fiercely and sinking rapidly, gave the order to abandon ship. Four life rafts were dropped. The depth charges were all checked to ensure safe settings. Shortly thereafter the *Walke* sank bow first. About one minute later, the depth charges exploded, killing and injuring many men, who, otherwise would have survived.

—LIEUTENANT W. J. COLLUM JR., USS *WALKE*, 30 NOVEMBER 1942

battleship closed with Kondō's powerful bombardment group, the power went out again.

At 2358, the moon set and a deeper darkness descended over Ironbottom Sound. Kondō's lookouts initially mistook the *South Dakota* for a cruiser, but all doubt about her identity vanished when four searchlights from his flagship *Atago* fixed on her a minute later. The *Kirishima* and two heavy cruisers immediately opened fire. The latter were at point-blank range, just 5,000 yards away. The Japanese battleship remained more distant, around 11,000 yards. One of her 14-inch shells slammed into the barbette of the *South Dakota*'s after turret, tearing a gash in nearby deck planks and scouring the armor. Eight-inch shells from the *Atago* and *Takao* tore into the *South Dakota*'s superstructure, damaging lightly protected installations and complicating her electrical problems. Kimura's screening destroyers fired torpedoes.

The heavy cruiser *Atago* steams at 34.12 knots during full power trials between the Tateyama mile posts on 25 August 1939. She has just been modernized. The *Atago* was the flagship of Vice Admiral Kondō's Emergency Bombardment Group and fought with the battleship *South Dakota* at close range, hitting her several times with 8-inch shells from her main battery. (U.S. Naval Institute Photo Archive)

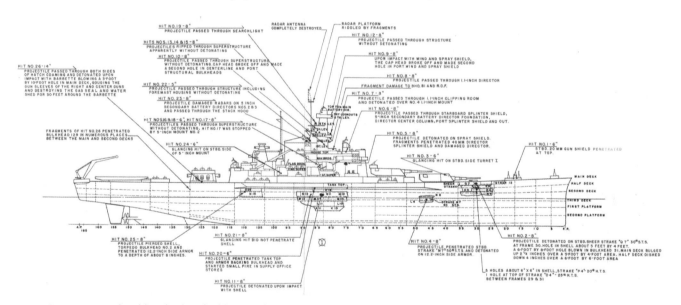

Damage received by the battleship *South Dakota* at the Second Naval Battle of Guadalcanal. Note the numerous 8-inch hits from the Japanese cruisers *Atago* and *Takao*. The battleship *Kirishima* was responsible for the 14-inch hits. The concentrated fire on the *South Dakota*'s superstructure knocked out control positions and disabled radars. (*War Damage Report No. 57*)

The heavy cruiser *Takao* on high speed trials in 1932. She was capable of making 35 knots. Note the large plume of water astern and the substantial bow wave. (U.S. Naval Institute Photo Archive)

This photograph shows "Hit No. 2" from the *South Dakota*'s damage report diagram. It is from an 8-inch shell that exploded against the hull and blew a hole in the starboard side. A larger hole was made in the bulkhead beyond. (National Archives)

On board the *South Dakota*, the damage mounted. A shell tore through the radar plot, wrecking the equipment. The main battery director was jammed in train, so target designation responsibilities shifted to the unprotected sky control. Communication with sky control was lost a few minutes later. The secondary conning position was hit. Radar and radio antennas were shot away. The *South Dakota*'s secondary battery opened fire, but her main battery remained silent. Her gunners were unable to get a solution on Kondō's ships.

One 16-inch salvo was fired by the main battery at 0007, but none of the spotters were able to see whether it was on target or not. The *South Dakota* had been rendered blind and practically helpless.

The location of the *Washington* was not known. Radio communication had failed. Radar plot had been demolished. Main battery Director 2 radar was the only radar functioning. Three fire control radars had been damaged by shells, and Number 4 secondary was inoperative due to electrical troubles. Many dead and wounded had been reported by Battle Station 2 as well as sky control. Turret 3 reported difficulty in train although it believed that it could still fire.

—CAPTAIN THOMAS L. GATCH, USS *SOUTH DAKOTA*, 24 NOVEMBER 1942

The battleship *Washington* is pictured off New York City on 21 August 1942, before her dispatch to the South Pacific. The *Washington* was Rear Admiral Lee's flagship for most of the war, and he commanded Task Group 64 from her the night of 14–15 November 1942. Note her many radars and compact superstructure. (National Archives)

Kondō was on the verge of destroying one of the Navy's most powerful ships, but he had run out of time. Lee's flagship the *Washington* had been tracking the *Kirishima* since 2335. Initially, he was hesitant to open fire. The admiral wanted to be certain the target was an enemy ship and not the *South Dakota*. The *Washington*'s SG radar was mounted on the front of the main battery control tower; it had a large blind spot to the rear. The *South Dakota* had been in that blind spot when the battleships were cruising in line, but she had since drifted out to starboard. Was she the "target" his gunners were tracking? Lee was unsure. He kept his guns silent while he attempted to clarify the situation.

When the *Atago*'s searchlights came on and the *South Dakota* was clearly illuminated in their brilliant beams, all doubt in Lee's mind immediately vanished as he recognized her silhouette. The *Washington*'s target was Japanese, and she was firing on the *South Dakota*. Lee gave the order to open fire. Commander Harvey Walsh, the *Washington*'s gunnery officer, put his team into action. The firing keys on the director closed, and as the *Washington*'s roll leveled out, her gyrostabilized director completed the firing circuit. Nine "superheavy" 2,700-pound armor piercing shells left their tubes in a blinding flash. Captain Davis summarized the moment:

In the second phase target had been tracked by radar ranges and bearing and later by optical train. Fire was opened at 8400 yards and a hit was probably obtained on first salvo and certainly on the second. Fire was rapid, on one turret ready light, for about two minutes thirty-nine seconds, firing about thirty-nine rounds. It was interrupted for one and a half minutes due to an erroneous report that target was sunk, and resumed for two minutes and forty-five seconds, during which time thirty-six rounds were fired. A total of seventy-five rounds were fired on this tar-

get which was believed to be an old type battleship. Starshell illumination was used on this phase after about the second salvo, sixty-two rounds being fired.

—CAPTAIN GLENN B. DAVIS, USS *WASHINGTON*, 27 NOVEMBER 1942

The *Kirishima* withered under the *Washington*'s accurate fire. Walsh and his assistant gunnery officer, Lieutenant Commander Edwin B. Hooper, used visual bearings and radar ranges to secure the maximum number of hits. Shells slammed into the *Kirishima*'s towering foremast; others penetrated her hull, their bursts appearing as a dull red glow inside the ship. Captain Iwabuchi turned to port, away from the incoming shells, but it brought no respite. Turret 2 was destroyed. Hits threatened the after magazines, and the executive officer, Commander Koro Ono, gave the order to flood them, silencing Turrets 3 and 4. The *Kirishima*'s last main battery turret stopped firing when the magazine for Turret 1, also threatened by the fires, was deliberately flooded. Hits on the starboard side created a significant list. Damage control parties counter flooded to correct it. The rudder stopped responding and jammed. After the *Washington* ceased fire, the *Kirishima* began an uncontrolled circle to port.

The counterflooding helped bring the ship back onto an even keel, but the starboard list continued to increase. Soon, it was difficult to stand upright on the deck. Captain Iwabuchi struggled to beach his ship and keep her from sinking, but he was unable to steer the *Kirishima* to safety. Two of Kimura's destroyers came alongside to take off the crew. To make the process easier, the port engine room was flooded to counteract the starboard list. As water poured into the compartment, the *Kirishima* lost stability and suddenly lurched to port. Tons of water which had been resting against the starboard side of her middle decks surged to the other side of the ship. The force was too much. In

The battleship *Kirishima* photographed in Sukumo Bay in 1937. Note her large forward superstructure, typical of Japanese World War II battleships, and the floatplane between her two after turrets. The *Kirishima* fought in both night actions in November, damaging several Navy ships the night of 12–13 November and hitting the *South Dakota* two nights later. She was crippled and left in a sinking condition by gunfire from the battleship *Washington*. (Naval History and Heritage Command)

UNITED STATES NAVAL INSTITUTE

The Sinking of the *Kirishima*

Following the Fourth Heavy Cruiser Division, we commenced firing on an enemy battleship [*South Dakota*] at the range of about 10,000 meters immediately after heavy cruiser *Atago* started her searchlight illuminations. Enemy gunfire also concentrated on us and inflicted more than six hits.

Fire started at various sections, while the fore radio room was destroyed, hydrometers of Number 3 and 4 turrets stopped, and the rudder developed trouble.

On the other hand, our first salvos of the main and secondary batteries made hits upon two enemy battleships: Two of the main battery's first salvo made hits and especially one of them blew off the enemy bridge. At least ten hits were made upon them, but the enemy could not be finished off. At 0049 the distance between us and them was increased.

By this time most of the fires were brought under control, and all engines were still operable with their full power, but the steering gear room was completely flooded, so we couldn't make way at all. In the meantime, the engine rooms became intolerable because of the increased heat, and most of the engineers were killed though they had been ordered to evacuate. Only the central engine could make the slowest speed.

Then fires once brought under control gained strength again, so that the fore and aft magazines became endangered. Orders to flood them were then issued.

As the light cruiser *Nagara* happened to close in, we asked her to tow our ship, but a negative answer was given. An attempt to prevent the flooding of the steering gear room also failing, the ship became hopeless.

—KIRISHIMA ACTION REPORT, 16 NOVEMBER 1942, FROM FADING VICTORY: THE DIARY OF ADMIRAL MATOME UGAKI, 1941–1945 (NAVAL INSTITUTE PRESS, 2008)

moments, the *Kirishima* capsized to port. As she rolled, her superstructure narrowly avoided crashing into the destroyer *Teruzuki*. Lieutenant Commander Tsurukichi Ikeda, in charge of the *Kirishima*'s secondary battery, estimated that 20 major-caliber hits had slammed into the ship. If so, Walsh and Hooper had delivered the most accurate sequence of battleship gunfire ever seen in combat. Regardless of the total number of hits, the *Washington*'s gunfire left the Japanese battleship mortally wounded within seven short minutes.

Lee quickly moved to exploit his victory. Kondō's formation—disrupted by the mortal wounding of the *Kirishima*—was confused and disorganized. Lee maintained a northwesterly course, toward the approaching Japanese transports. When they recognized the threat, the Japanese cruisers and some of Kimura's destroyers took off in pursuit. Lee's bold maneuver took them away from the *South Dakota* and allowed Captain Gatch to extricate his crippled battleship from danger.

Washington was undamaged but *South Dakota* having been the principal target for the enemy fire was badly cut up about the topside by numerous 8-in, 6-in, and 5.5-in hits. Two 14-in hits were defeated by *South Dakota*'s armor without causing serious damage. As a result of enemy fire *South Dakota* lost all radio communications, both search radars, all but one fire control radar, and suffered extensive damage to directors and fire control circuits. Recognizing the fact that above damage had reduced his ship from an asset to a liability the Commanding Officer of the *South*

Another view of the *Takao*, this time on 14 July 1939, after her reconstruction. She is running trials and making 34.25 knots on the measured mile off Tateyama. The combination of the high speed and her low freeboard aft is causing water to come up over her stern. (U.S. Naval Institute Photo Archive)

Dakota, at 0010, wisely decided to retire—to the great relief of the Task Force Commander.

—REAR ADMIRAL WILLIS A. LEE, COMMANDER TF 64, 18 FEBRUARY 1943

Lee pushed the *Washington* ahead, changing course to north by northwest, clearly making for the path of the transports. Observing the situation on the SG radar display, Lee commented that his change of course "appeared to set the whole enemy field in motion to the north and northwest." He maintained that course for ten minutes while the Japanese destroyers launched torpedoes—some of which exploded in the battleship's wake—and attempted to regroup, laying a smokescreen to the northeast. From afar, Vice Admiral Ugaki monitored communications from Kondo's force with growing apprehension. The situation did not appear to be going well.

> At 0047 we received the following urgent telegram from the commander, advanced force: "Guadalcanal attack force and the reinforcements are engaging with two new type enemy battleships and several cruisers and destroyers off Lunga at 0018. Tonight's shore bombardment called off." Then the commander, advance force, ordered the convoy to go aground and *Kirishima* to withdraw towards the north. The situation didn't seem favorable. Later, the following telegrams were received in succession: "At 0104 we are going to withdraw towards the north after rearranging the battlefield." "Those who are pursuing the enemy should carry out attacks and then withdraw towards the north." "Report the condition of *Kirishima*."

—14 NOVEMBER 1942, FROM *FADING VICTORY: THE DIARY OF ADMIRAL MATOME UGAKI, 1941–1945* (NAVAL INSTITUTE PRESS, 2008)

As the *Washington* approached a rain squall that looked like another destroyer smokescreen, Captain Davis made a sharp change of course to avoid it. Lee ordered the *Washington* to continue through the turn and retire south. He correctly estimated that his advance to the northwest had delayed the transports. Tanaka had reversed course to avoid contact with Lee's flagship.

CACTUS TRIUMPHANT

Lee's victory doomed the last determined Japanese effort to retake Guadalcanal. His "scratch team" had entered Savo Sound with resolve and a clear objective, to stop the bombardment of Henderson Field. Although the use of battleships in narrow waters was a great risk, he had deftly used his destroyers to screen his heavy ships and identify potential targets. He praised their performance:

> In breaking up the enemy destroyer attack our destroyers certainly relieved the battleships of a serious hazard and probably saved their bacon. Formed only the night before, composed of one destroyer from each of four different divisions, and led by the senior skipper (T. E. Frazier, late Commander, U.S. Navy, Commanding Officer, *Walke*), the destroyers of TF 64 put up a fight of which any veteran division might well be proud. Lacking any SG radars, and three of the four having no gunnery radar, they nevertheless outgunned a superior number of Japanese destroyers almost invisible against the loom of Savo Island.

—REAR ADMIRAL WILLIS A. LEE, COMMANDER TF 64, 18 FEBRUARY 1943

Although Lee's destroyers had not, in fact, outgunned Kimura's screening unit, they had performed a valuable service in absorbing the brunt of their torpedo attack. The *Walke*, *Benham*, *Gwin*, and *Preston* had prevented the battleships from becoming embroiled in a confused melee, allowing Lee to make the most of his superiority in large-caliber gunfire. Even though the *South Dakota* had been crippled and blinded, the *Washington* maintained situational awareness and opened fire at the critical moment. The gunfire of Lee's flagship—honed to a high standard by his personal leadership—won the Second Naval Battle of Guadalcanal and guaranteed the survival of the aviators at Henderson Field.

Lee recognized that his victory had been a narrow one, noting that "we have no edge on the Japanese in experience, skill, training, or permanence of personnel." But thanks to the efforts of his men, on the morning of 15 November 1942, the Americans did possess a significant edge: dominance of the skies over Guadalcanal. Adrift in Ironbottom Sound, the survivors of the destroyers *Preston* and *Walke* had a ringside seat for the final approach of the remaining Japanese transports, the *Hirokawa Maru*, *Kinugawa Maru*, *Yamaura Maru*, and *Yamazuki Maru*.

> Early in the morning of November 15, 1942, *Preston* survivors in the water between Savo Island and Cape Esperance . . . saw the following events: All times are approximate and are zone -12. At about daybreak (0530) four enemy cargo ships, each of from 3000 to 5000 tons, approached Cape Esperance from the westward. These vessels came in close to the beach and headed for Lunga Point. They were spotted by

100   UNITED STATES NAVAL INSTITUTE

Admiral William F. Halsey presents the Navy Cross to Rear Admiral Willis A. Lee in January 1943. Lee was awarded the decoration because of his successful defense of Henderson Field during the Second Naval Battle of Guadalcanal. (National Archives)

our dive bombers and in a short while were being attacked. Details of the bombing could not be seen but all four vessels were observed to catch fire, and continued to burn. There was one large explosion near one of the vessels but whether it was on the beach or on the ship could not be seen. At about 0930 a destroyer (later identified as the *Meade* [DD-602]) came from the eastward and fired at each of the ships. The enemy ships did not return the fire. In a short time, all of the enemy ships were burning fiercely and were still burning when the survivors from the *Preston* were picked up about 1430.

—LIEUTENANT (JUNIOR GRADE) W. W. WOODS, USS *PRESTON*, 30 NOVEMBER 1942

Not surprisingly, Lieutenant (junior grade) Woods and his fellow survivors had an imprecise sense of time. The transports entered Savo Sound and beached at about 0400. At about the same time, both airfields on Guadalcanal came to life. On the fighter strip, a taxiing fighter drew the attention of Japanese artillery. Periodic shelling would continue throughout the day as the Japanese attempted to disrupt aerial operations and ensure the survival of the troops and supplies aboard the transports.

The first planes to strike the transports were eight Marine dive bombers led by Major Joe Sailer; they struck two ships that had beached at Tassafaronga.

A second wave of bombers attacked soon thereafter. Seaplanes from retiring Japanese ships attempted to interfere with these strikes, but they could only offer token resistance. An attack later that morning delighted the survivors of the *Walke*.

At 0730, several friendly dive bombers from Henderson Field, Guadalcanal, circled over the four enemy ships, and made attacks on same. All four ships were hit and set on fire. One plane scored a direct hit on a pile of material on shore, which material blew up, sending a great column of flame and smoke about 300 feet in the air. Said material was believed to be ammunition. Shortly thereafter, the planes returned to Henderson Field, leaving the four enemy vessels blazing.

—LIEUTENANT W. J. COLLUM JR., USS *WALKE*, 30 NOVEMBER 1942

The nearest transport was close enough to be hit by Vandegrift's artillery. The men of Battery F of the 244th Coast Artillery dragged two of their 155-mm guns to the beach and trained their sights on her hull. Marine 5-inch guns from the 3d Defense Battalion also joined in. Soon, these shells were finding their mark.

Although the four remaining transports had not been stopped, the Japanese resupply effort was effectively thwarted. Much of what was delivered to the island was consumed in explosions and fires on the beaches

The destroyer *Meade* photographed off New York City on 20 June 1942, during her delivery from the Bethlehem Steel Company. The *Meade* entered Ironbottom Sound the morning of 15 November 1942, and, finding no enemy warships covering the Japanese transports, attacked them and supply dumps ashore. Navy sailors in the water who observed the *Meade* cheered. (National Archives)

as American aviators and artillerymen subjected the supplies and transports to a relentless bombardment. The destroyer *Meade*, cheered on by the *Preston*'s survivors, also contributed by shelling the Japanese ships and their supply dumps ashore. Rear Admiral Raymond A. Spruance, Nimitz's chief of staff, praised the *Meade*'s aggressiveness: "As the only combatant ship in the area on 15 November, *Meade* exercised control of the sea and destroyed the beached enemy ships at her leisure."

Like Spruance, Vice Admiral Ugaki, assessed the impact of combat operations from afar. He was frustrated that two of the IJN's battleships had been lost in the effort to retake the island. Ugaki attributed the *Kirishima*'s destruction to a numerical imbalance; she had been outnumbered and outgunned.

Battleship *Kirishima* fought two enemy battleships, one of which was a *North Carolina* type, and was seriously damaged. A torpedo hit [actually the *Washington*'s shells] on her stern made her steering impossible, and she was flooded. She tried once to reach Camimbo at her slowest speed, but there seemed to be no prospect of using the engine as ninety percent of the engine room crew were killed. All hands were transferred to destroyers. We thereupon sent a telegram leaving her disposal to the discretion of the commander, advance force. At 0335 she capsized and sank at a point 8.5 miles bearing 285 degrees of the summit of Savo Island.

—15 NOVEMBER 1942, FROM *FADING VICTORY: THE DIARY OF ADMIRAL MATOME UGAKI, 1941–1945*

The loss of the *Hiei* was a more significant blow. It was particularly devastating to Vice Admiral Abe.

Vice Admiral Abe, commander, Eleventh Battleship Division, came on board at 1000. He looked sad with a bandage over his lower jaw. With a sorrowful face he reported losing two ships under his command. The feelings of those who come back after losing their ship in battle are always the same. He seemed to suffer especially for his sunken *Hiei*. He even confided that he thought he would have been better to have gone down with *Hiei*. I can well appreciate how he felt.

—17 NOVEMBER 1942, FROM *FADING VICTORY: THE DIARY OF ADMIRAL MATOME UGAKI, 1941–1945* (NAVAL INSTITUTE PRESS, 2008)

Although significant, IJN officers felt these losses would have been an acceptable cost for retaking Guadalcanal and regaining the initiative in the South Pacific. However, Rear Admiral Tanaka's assessment that just 2,000 troops and limited supplies were delivered to the island made it clear that his convoy would not achieve that goal.

Halsey's determination to "throw punches" and aggressively seek action with the Japanese had finally given U.S. forces the upper hand. Although Callaghan's battle had been a tactical draw, his desperate sacrifice changed the strategic situation. He preserved the airfields and allowed American aviators to decimate Tanaka's reinforcement convoy, forcing Kondō to plan a second bombardment. This gave Lee the opportunity to intervene decisively. With his victory, the airmen were able to decimate the Japanese reinforcement effort, dooming their final push to retake Guadalcanal.

The *Kinugawa Maru* rests off Tassafaronga Point, where she beached and sank on 15 November 1942. Savo Island is in the distance on the right. This picture was taken a year later, in November 1943 (National Archives)

The *Yamazuki Maru* rests off Guadalcanal, beached and burnt out after aerial attacks on 15 November 1942. She is pictured on 15 February 1943. (National Archives)

CONCLUSION

AFTER THE DEFEAT IN NOVEMBER, THE JAPANESE CONSIDERED THEIR OPTIONS.
Although some officers remained optimistic that Guadalcanal could be retaken, more realistic views began to be considered, particularly among those who had visited the island. It was becoming clear that the IJN could not match Halsey's regular reinforcement efforts. On 21 November, Vice Admiral Ugaki noted that two American transports had arrived off Guadalcanal that morning, and that by 7 December "two or three transports were unloading daily." Guadalcanal was on its way to becoming a major U.S. base. Ugaki and other IJN officers advocated shifting their defensive efforts to New Guinea and other islands of the Solomon chain, closer to Rabaul. The high command initially resisted these efforts; Ugaki blamed the army's intransigence.

A Marine examines a wrecked Japanese landing craft on the Guadalcanal shore on 23 March 1943. It had been destroyed by fire from Marine half-tracks during the fighting of the previous year. (National Archives)

A great change, the strategic policy for abandoning Guadalcanal and securing Eastern New Guinea, won't be easy because of the army's stubbornness. Nevertheless, if any more useless attritions are added up after repeating desperate struggles, some break will surely take place elsewhere in our national defense. So I requested the senior staff officer to determine the limit of terms beyond which the recapture of Guadalcanal would be impossible, with the aim of taking necessary timely steps.

—26 NOVEMBER 1942, FROM *FADING VICTORY: THE DIARY OF ADMIRAL MATOME UGAKI, 1941–1945* (NAVAL INSTITUTE PRESS, 2008)

The Imperial Army reorganized their defenses of the southern Pacific in November. General Hitoshi Imamura's 8th Area Army was created on the 16th, with responsibility for Hyakutake's 17th Army on Guadalcanal and Lieutenant General Hatazō Adachi's newly created 18th Army in New Guinea. Imamura was determined to recapture Guadalcanal and resolved to bring two more divisions to the island in February 1943. In the meantime, efforts to resupply the 17th Army became more and more difficult. Cactus pilots attacked the Tokyo Express runs during the day, and Halsey was determined to stop them at night.

As Rear Admiral Tanaka prepared to resupply Japanese forces on Guadalcanal with eight destroyers on 29 November, Halsey ordered the new commander of TF 67, Rear Admiral Carleton H. Wright, to intercept. Wright had the heavy cruisers *Minneapolis* (CA-36), *New Orleans* (CA-32), *Northampton* (CA-26), and *Pensacola* (CA-24) along with light cruiser *Honolulu* (CL-48) and destroyers *Fletcher*, *Drayton* (DD-366), *Maury* (DD-401), and *Perkins* (DD-377). As they entered Ironbottom Sound the evening of 30 November, Halsey ordered two more destroyers, *Lamson*

(DD-367) and *Lardner* (DD-487), to join Wright's force. They took station at the rear of the formation.

Wright inherited a battle plan crafted by Rear Admiral Kinkaid. Kinkaid's plan relied on the van

SHIPS ENGAGED AND LOSSES— NAVAL BATTLE OF GUADALCANAL

	USN		IJN	
	Engaged	Lost	Engaged	Lost
Battleships	2	0	2	2
Heavy Cruisers	3	0	6	1
Light Cruisers	3	2	4	0
Destroyers	16	7	36	3
Transports	7	0	11	11

INCLUDES SHIPS THAT ESCORTED THE RESPECTIVE CONVOYS BUT DID NOT FIGHT IN THE NIGHT BATTLES.

Pensacola *Torpedoed*, a painting by Clarence Joseph Tibado, a member of the ship's crew. Tibado's art captures the intensity of the fight to save the ship at the Battle of Tassafaronga. (National Museum of American History)

destroyers to make a surprise torpedo attack using the *Fletcher*'s SG radar, but as the Battle of Tassafaronga opened, Wright refused to give Commander Cole permission to launch torpedoes until it was too late. Almost immediately after doing so, and before the Cole's torpedoes could arrive among Tanaka's ships, Wright ordered his cruisers to open fire. Surprise was lost before any hits were scored.

Tanaka's force reacted as they had been trained. His chief of staff, Captain Yasumi Toyama, gave the signal for a mass torpedo attack. Although some ships struggled to cast off their supply drums—designed be released near the beach and float to shore—at least 44 Type 93 torpedoes were soon streaming toward Wright's cruisers. *Takanami* was closest to the cruiser line and presented the best radar target. Several ships concentrated upon her; multiple shell hits set the *Takanami* ablaze and left her in a sinking condition. Tanaka's other destroyers—the *Naganami*, *Makinami*, *Kuroshio*, *Oyashio*, *Kagerō*, *Kawakaze*, and *Suzukaze*—fired torpedoes and reversed course.

Their salvo of Long Lances devastated Wright's cruisers. He reported that "*Minneapolis* was struck by two torpedoes. . . . Almost simultaneously the *New Orleans* . . . was struck by at least one. . . . Both ships had their bows blown off and the two ships and the surrounding ocean were a mass of flame from the gasoline in their forward storage tanks. . . . *Minneapolis*, although apparently sinking, continued to fire all turret guns until power failed." The *Pensacola* was also hit and flames engulfed her mainmast. Two torpedoes struck the *Northampton*, opened her after engine room to the sea, and triggered intense fires that hindered damage control efforts. She sank within a few hours; Wright's other damaged cruisers limped to Tulagi. Only the *Honolulu* and the

Cruiser *New Orleans* lost her bow forward of turret two in the Battle of Tassafaronga the night of 30 November 1942. This is how she appeared after sailing stern first to Sydney, Australia in December. Note the FC radar above her main battery director. (National Archives)

The *New Orleans* Is Hit

Sparks and flames leapt over twice the height of the foremast, and a column of water was thrown up almost as high. It drenched the ship . . . . Within a second or two after the hit a second explosion occurred, which rocked the ship very severely with a loping motion. This was probably caused by turret one falling off. I felt certain that at least one of the forward magazines had gone. My . . . talkers called the bridge to ensure that they were functioning. Neither could get a reply, so I rang the steering alarm, shifting steering control to steering aft, and took over the conn. . . . [T]he *Honolulu* was passing our bow from starboard to port . . . and I had made up my mind to fall in astern of her and continue the engagement when a torpedo was reported on our starboard quarter. I then ordered the rudder put hard left and all engines ahead emergency full.

—COMMANDER WHITAKER F. RIGGS, EXECUTIVE OFFICER, USS *NEW ORLEANS*, 3 DECEMBER 1942

A beach near Cape Esperance is strewn with wrecked and abandoned Japanese landing craft, photographed in May 1943. (National Archives)

destroyers were unscathed. TF 67 had paid a high price, but they kept Tanaka from delivering any supplies to the 17th Army.

The Battle of Tassafaronga forced Halsey to rely on Tulagi-based PT boats and radar-equipped patrol planes to interfere with nocturnal Japanese resupply efforts. On 7 December, seven destroyers attempted to deliver troops and supplies to Guadalcanal. Consistent attacks by PT boats and planes forced them to turn back. Even submarines faced serious risks. On the night of 9 December, the submarine *I-3* attempted a resupply run and was caught on the surface by *PT-59*. Two torpedo hits ruptured *I-3*'s hull and sent her to the bottom. Two nights later, Tanaka made another attempt to bring food and ammunition. His ten destroyers were attacked by a collection of PT boats; the destroyer *Teruzuki* was hit and crippled. When flames reached a magazine early that morning, they triggered an explosion that destroyed the ship.

The Japanese situation on Guadalcanal became progressively more desperate. U.S. patrols, malnutrition, and disease were steadily reducing the number of combat-ready troops. While the Japanese grew weaker, the strength of U.S. forces steadily increased. On 9 December, Major General Alexander M. Patch, U.S.

Army, arrived and relieved General Vandegrift. By the end of the month, 8,000 fresh officers and men of the 25th Infantry Division had augmented Patch's command. He transitioned from aggressive patrolling to major offensive operations. The Japanese had very little strength left to resist these moves; disease was decimating their numbers.

> Out of 3000 men of one regiment, now only sixty to seventy remain capable of continuing to fight. The present strength fit to fight is only 4200 altogether. About 1500 men a month are being lost. They are putting up a gallant fight in position, but they are suffering forty to fifty casualties daily due to enemy bombing and gunfire. Less than one-third are fit for combat, while the rest are sick and wounded. Most of them are suffering from beriberi and malaria, and the losses due to those diseases reach two to three times those by enemy bombing and bombardment.

—REPORT OF MAJOR TAKAHIKO HYASHI, 8 DECEMBER 1942, FROM *FADING VICTORY: THE DIARY OF ADMIRAL MATOME UGAKI, 1941–1945*

The evidence was clear. Despite Imamura's desire to recapture the island, the Japanese presence on Guadalcanal was unsustainable. By 26 December, the high commands of the IJN and Imperial Army had agreed to

Operation KE—The Beginning of the End

Operation KE was a watershed moment of the Pacific War: the end of the beginning and the beginning of the end. On the one hand, it marked the end of the Guadalcanal campaign—a blood-drenched saga that had begun six months before with the landing of the 1st Marines on Beach Red. On the other hand, Operation KE heralded the beginning of an agonizing retreat back across the Pacific—an odyssey of death and destruction that finally ended for Dai Nippon Teikoku Kaigun two and a half years later in Tokyo Bay on the deck of the USS *Missouri*.

—ROGER & DENNIS LETOURNEAU, *OPERATION KE: THE CACTUS AIR FORCE AND THE JAPANESE WITHDRAWAL FROM GUADALCANAL* (NAVAL INSTITUTE PRESS, 2012)

abandon the island; on 31 December, Emperor Hirohito endorsed this view. Ugaki recorded the decision in his diary: "Guadalcanal is now hopeless." Plans to evacuate the garrison were set in motion.

Operation KE was another large, complex plan, but this time, instead of attempting to reinforce Guadalcanal, the Japanese withdrew their troops. During the nights of 1, 4, and 7 February, Mikawa's destroyers evacuated some 10,600 men from the island. One destroyer—the *Makigumo*—was lost during the second evacuation run when she hit a mine while attempting to avoid PT boats. Cactus flyers harassed the Japanese ships, damaging the destroyers *Makinami* (1 February) and *Isokaze* (7 February), but failed to prevent the convoys from reaching Guadalcanal. Japanese pilots had more success; Bettys and Nells from Rabaul struck Rear Admiral Robert C. Giffen's TF 18 the night of 29 January at the Battle of Rennell Island. The cruiser *Chicago* was hit by two torpedoes. The next afternoon, while the tug *Navajo* (AT-64) attempted to tow her to safety, another flight of Japanese torpedo bombers attacked. Several more torpedoes hit the cruiser, and 20 minutes later, the *Chicago* went down.

Halsey and other Allied commanders assumed the Japanese high-speed runs were reinforcement missions and acted accordingly, holding major naval forces in reserve ready to thwart a major thrust like that in mid-November. Had they realized the destroyers were evacuating the garrison, they would have been much more aggressive. On 8 February, as Patch's men advanced, they encountered no resistance. He quickly realized that the Japanese missions over the past week had evacuated their forces. By late afternoon the next day, two of Patch's columns met up at the village of Tenaro near Cape Esperance. They had seized the

Admiral Halsey and Major General Vandegrift confer at Halsey's headquarters in Nouméa in January 1943. Although neither man realized it yet, the Japanese had given up attempting to retake Guadalcanal and were making plans to withdraw. (Naval History and Heritage Command)

Admiral King (right), the initiator of the Guadalcanal campaign, and Admiral Halsey, its victor, flank Secretary of the Navy Frank Knox at the Navy Department, Washington, D.C., in January 1944. Halsey has just been awarded a gold star in lieu of a second Distinguished Service Medal. (National Archives)

shoreline surrounding former Japanese positions. Patch sent Halsey a message that concluded, "the Tokyo Express no longer has a terminus on Guadalcanal." The campaign for Guadalcanal was over.

Victory at Guadalcanal secured the strategic initiative for Admiral Nimitz and his Pacific Fleet. For the remainder of the war, the Japanese would be on the defensive. Nimitz and his subordinates initiated a series of determined offensives, that, together with General Douglas MacArthur's thrust in the Southwest Pacific, shattered the Japanese defensive perimeter, overwhelmed their naval forces, and ultimately brought the war to a successful conclusion in August 1945. That process began with the first offensive—Operation Watchtower—in which the Navy deliberately accepted inadequate preparations in order to seize the opportunity presented by the victory at Midway. Along with the demands of other theaters across the globe, "Operation Shoestring"

taxed the Navy and Marine Corps to their limits. Victory resulted from an emphasis on the principles embedded in the Navy's prewar tactical doctrine: aggressive action, quick and effective gunfire, and decentralized command and control.

The emphasis on aggressive action was central to Halsey's decision to "punch" and proactively thwart Japanese efforts to overwhelm Guadalcanal's defenses. He recognized that continual pressure would create opportunities for his subordinates and trusted them to take advantage. Vandegrift did so by actively defending his perimeter, using patrols and spoiling attacks to disrupt Japanese preparations, destroy their supplies, and keep them off balance. Although Scott fought at Cape Esperance before Halsey took command, his bold plan to intercept Gotō's bombardment force and end the IJN's dominance of the waters off Guadalcanal reflected Halsey's approach to leadership and the Navy's tactical principles. Scott's plan leveraged gunfire and

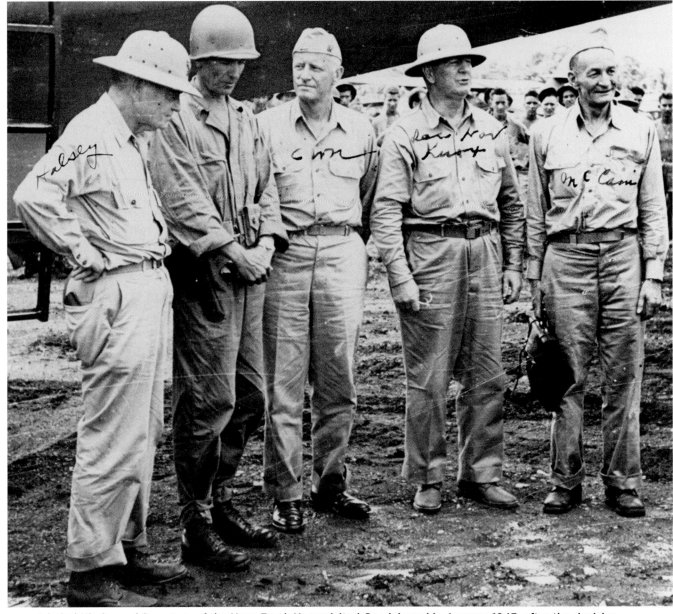

Admiral Nimitz and Secretary of the Navy Frank Knox visited Guadalcanal in January 1943, after the decisive victories of the previous November. Pictured here (left to right) are: Admiral Halsey, an unidentified Marine officer, Admiral Nimitz, Knox, and Rear Admiral McCain. The handwriting on the photo is Nimitz's. (Naval History and Heritage Command)

new tactical ideas that he had personally developed. Callaghan followed this pattern when he aggressively sought out Abe's bombardment unit and brought his flagship the *San Francisco* to decisive range, disrupting the Japanese formation's cohesion and preventing the bombardment of Henderson Field. Lee devised a new approach and punched in his own way, using his destroyers to identify targets for his big guns. His tactical skill thwarted another bombardment and kept the Japanese transports as far as possible from their destination.

The Navy's tactical doctrine relied on individual creativity and incorporated a clear expectation. When confronted with opportunities, officers and men were expected to act with clear resolve, take advantage of the situation, and make the most of their capabilities. Scott, Callaghan, Lee, and the officers and men of their ships met this high bar. Although effective doctrine and training created the possibility for success in Ironbottom Sound, it was countless acts of courage that secured it. Halsey acknowledged this when, after his promotion to the rank of full admiral,

The *Chicago* Is Torpedoed

At 1931, a fresh flight of Bettys drove in from the east. One torpedo passed just ahead of *Chicago* and another hit *Louisville* solidly, but failed to detonate. Several planes were hit, some reportedly shot down. At 1938, a more determined group swooped in. One attacker blew up astern of *Waller*, revealing another, flaming brightly, which dove across *Chicago*'s bow, searing the forecastle with burning gasoline, before crashing into the water. At 1945, the next wave scored a torpedo hit in *Chicago*'s starboard side, immediately flooding two compartments and pouring water into the after fireroom. Three of her four propeller shafts came to a stop and she lost steering control. A few moments later a second torpedo hit her No. 3 Fire room, halting the shaft and bringing the big ship to a stop. *Louisville* kicked up to 30 knots to swing clear of the damaged ship, then circled astern to lend protection. Minutes later, a final torpedo smashed into *Wichita*—luckily, it did not explode.

—RUSSELL SYDNOR CRENSHAW JR., *SOUTH PACIFIC DESTROYER* (NAVAL INSTITUTE PRESS, 1998)

---

he mailed his vice admiral insignia to the widows of Callaghan and Scott. With the packages he included notes explaining to each woman that the bravery of her husband had secured Halsey his promotion to admiral. It was a fair assessment. Arguably the most important moment in the campaign came in the early morning hours of 13 November, when the two rear admirals took their 13 ships into the heart of a much more powerful enemy formation and tore it apart, a tactical gambit that cost them their lives. Both were posthumously awarded the Medal of Honor.

They were not the only ones to display exceptional bravery that night. Lieutenant Commanders Bruce McCandless and Herbert E. Schonland were also awarded the Medal of Honor for their part in keeping the *San Francisco* afloat and conning her to safety. In a piece written soon after the war, McCandless made a point of highlighting the courage of his shipmates. In "The Valiant Men of USS *San Francisco*," published in the mid-April 1957 issue of *Our Navy*, McCandless recalled the efforts of "enlisted men and junior officers" on board his ship. He cited mess attendants, quartermasters, boatswain's mates, carpenters, and Marines who fought to save their ship or sacrificed themselves for their shipmates. McCandless highlighted the heroism of Boatswain's Mate First Class Reinhardt J. Keppler in particular. McCandless called Keppler's gallantry "representative of the actions of many others." It was, and not just on board the *San Francisco*. Even in the dry style typical of U.S. Navy action reports, the desperate nature of the fighting—and the individual acts of heroism—shine through, a fact not lost on Rear Admiral Spruance as he read through them.

> In the actions covered by this report there were many inspiring instances of sound judgment and cool reaction under heavy fire. I can only admire the courage of our crews in action, their determination under fire, and the tenacity with which they fought fire and damage so as to overcome what appeared to be impossible obstacles in saving their ships. . . . This series of engagements, both immediately and in far reaching results, well deserves the name of the Battle of the Solomons. In four days, the fate of Guadalcanal and the fate of our campaign in the South Pacific for months to come were decided. There were many courageous decisions, from lowest to highest commands, and heroic actions without number.

—REAR ADMIRAL R. A. SPRUANCE, DEPUTY COMMANDER, PACIFIC FLEET, 18 FEBRUARY 1943

The Navy triumphed at Guadalcanal for two reasons. Effective tactical principles developed before the war provided a foundation for success, while bold individual decisions by officers and men capitalized on momentary opportunities. Together, the combination of these two was enough. They secured tactical victory at Cape Esperance and strategic victory in mid-November 1942, allowing U.S. land and aerial forces to dominate the island and the skies above it. Further Japanese resistance proved futile, beginning a long pattern of sustained defeat in the Pacific.

Reinhardt J. Keppler

Medal of Honor Citation

For extraordinary heroism and distinguished courage above and beyond the call of duty while serving aboard the USS *San Francisco* during action against enemy Japanese forces in the Solomon Islands, 12-13 November 1942. When a hostile torpedo plane, during a daylight air raid, crashed on the after machine-gun platform, Keppler promptly assisted in the removal of the dead and, by his capable supervision of the wounded, undoubtedly helped save the lives of several shipmates who otherwise might have perished. That night, when the hangar was set afire during the great battle off Savo Island, he bravely led a hose into the starboard side of the stricken area and there, without assistance and despite frequent hits from terrific enemy bombardment, eventually brought the fire under control. Later, although mortally wounded, he labored valiantly in the midst of bursting shells, persistently directing fire-fighting operations and administrating to wounded personnel until he finally collapsed from loss of blood, aged 24. His great personal valor, maintained with utter disregard of personal safety, was in keeping with the highest traditions of the U. S. Naval Service. He gallantly gave his life for his country.

Norman Scott

Medal of Honor Citation

For extraordinary heroism and conspicuous intrepidity above and beyond the call of duty during action against enemy Japanese forces off Savo Island on the night of 11-12 October and again on the night of 12-13 November 1942. In the earlier action, intercepting a Japanese Task Force intent upon storming our island positions and landing reinforcements at Guadalcanal, Rear Adm. Scott, with courageous skill and superb coordination of the units under his command, destroyed eight hostile vessels and put the others to flight. Again challenged, a month later, by the return of a stubborn and persistent foe, he led his force into a desperate battle against tremendous odds, directing close-range operations against the invading enemy until he himself was killed in the furious bombardment by their superior firepower. On each of these occasions his dauntless initiative, inspiring leadership and judicious foresight in a crisis of grave responsibility contributed decisively to the rout of a powerful invasion fleet and to the consequent frustration of a formidable Japanese offensive. He gallantly gave his life in the service of his country.

Daniel J. Callaghan

Medal of Honor Citation

For extraordinary heroism and conspicuous intrepidity above and beyond the call of duty during action against enemy Japanese forces off Savo Island on the night of 12–13 November 1942. Although out-balanced in strength and numbers by a desperate and determined enemy, Rear Adm. Callaghan, with ingenious tactical skill and superb coordination of the units under his command, led his forces into battle against tremendous odds, thereby contributing decisively to the rout of a powerful invasion fleet, and to the consequent frustration of a formidable Japanese offensive. While faithfully directing close-range operations in the face of furious bombardment by superior enemy fire power, he was killed on the bridge of his flagship. His courageous initiative, inspiring leadership, and judicious foresight in a crisis of grave responsibility were in keeping with the finest traditions of the U.S. Naval Service. He gallantly gave his life in the defense of his country.

The battleship *Washington* maneuvers off Hawaii in mid-1943. Like the Navy's Pacific Fleet, the *Washington* emerged from the fighting off Guadalcanal triumphant and became more powerful as the lessons from that fighting were integrated into tactics and doctrine. (National Archives)

Herbert E. Schonland

Medal of Honor Citation

For extreme heroism and courage above and beyond the call of duty as damage control officer of the USS *San Francisco* in action against greatly superior enemy forces in the battle off Savo Island, 12–13 November 1942. In the same violent night engagement in which all of his superior officers were killed or wounded, Lt. Cdr. Schonland was fighting valiantly to free the *San Francisco* of large quantities of water flooding the second deck compartments through numerous shell holes caused by enemy fire. Upon being informed that he was commanding officer, he ascertained that the conning of the ship was being efficiently handled, then directed the officer who had taken over that task to continue while he himself resumed the vitally important work of maintaining the stability of the ship. In water waist deep, he carried on his efforts in darkness illuminated only by hand lanterns until water in flooded compartments had been drained or pumped off and watertight integrity had again been restored to the *San Francisco*. His great personal valor and gallant devotion to duty at great peril to his own life were instrumental in bringing his ship back to port under her own power, saved to fight again in the service of her country.

Bruce McCandless

Medal of Honor Citation

For conspicuous gallantry and exceptionally distinguished service above and beyond the call of duty as communication officer of the USS *San Francisco* in combat with enemy Japanese forces in the battle off Savo Island, 12–13 November 1942. In the midst of a violent night engagement, the fire of a determined and desperate enemy seriously wounded Lt. Cdr. McCandless and rendered him unconscious, killed or wounded the admiral in command, his staff, the captain of the ship, the navigator, and all other personnel on the navigating and signal bridges. Faced with the lack of superior command upon his recovery, and displaying superb initiative, he promptly assumed command of the ship and ordered her course and gunfire against an overwhelmingly powerful force. With his superiors in other vessels unaware of the loss of their admiral, and challenged by his great responsibility, Lt. Cdr. McCandless boldly continued to engage the enemy and to lead our column of following vessels to a great victory. Largely through his brilliant seamanship and great courage, the *San Francisco* was brought back to port, saved to fight again in the service of her country.

World of Warships is a free-to-play, naval warfare–themed, massively multiplayer online game produced and published by Wargaming. Like their other games, *World of Tanks* (WoT) and *World of Warplanes* (WoWP), players take control of historic vehicles to battle others in player-versus-player or play cooperatively against bots or in an advanced player-versus-environment (PvE) battle mode. *World of Warships* (WoWs) was originally released for PC in 2015; the PlayStation 4 and Xbox One console versions, titled *World of Warships: Legends*, followed in 2019, and it was released on the PlayStation 5 and Xbox Series X/S in April 2021.

Developed by Lesta Studios in St. Petersburg, Russia, *World of Warships* (PC) currently has more than 44 million registered players—playing on five main servers across the globe. More than 500 dedicated staff members work on a four-week update cycle to bring new features, ships, and mechanics to the game—keeping gameplay fresh and inviting to new players. The game features more than 400 ships, spread across 12 different in-game nations. Ships are designed based on historical documents and actual blueprints from the first half of the 20th century, and it takes from two to six man-months on average to create each of these ships. There are more than 20 ports to choose from, and 10 of them are re-created based on historical harbors and port towns.

Developed by the team behind *World of Warships* for PC, *World of Warships: Legends* is a completely new entry in Wargaming's flagship nautical franchise that takes full advantage of the power and capabilities of home consoles. *World of Warships: Legends* brings the online naval action loved by millions to home consoles for the very first time, alongside a host of content and features exclusive to the console experience. *World of Warships: Legends* is now available for download from the PlayStation® Store and Microsoft Store. Players can now wage wars across a variety of maps, in numerous warships, and enjoy stunning oceanic vistas with glorious HDR support on PlayStation®4 and Xbox One X. Full 4K support is available on PlayStation®4 Pro, PlayStation®5, and Xbox One X too! *Legends* also supports standard high-def on PlayStation®4 and Xbox One, with more intriguing graphics on the horizon.

Wargaming preserves naval history by making a series of documentaries on museum ships. Since 2014, Wargaming Saint Petersburg published 50 episodes devoted to the world's most popular museum ships in the United States, Great Britain, Canada, France, Japan, Germany, Greece, Australia, Sweden, Poland, Russian Federation, and China. Documentary videos cover all main classes of warships engaged in world wars such as aircraft carriers, battleships, cruisers, destroyers, and submarines. If you are interested in learning about the birth and development of U.S. naval aviation, please scan the QR-code below with your cell phone or simply find the respective video on YouTube by typing its name: "Naval Legends: Birth and Development of US Naval Aviation."